JB JOSSEY-BASS™
A Wiley Brand

94 Terrific Ways to Recruit Volunteers

SECOND EDITION

Scott C. Stevenson, Editor

WILEY

94 Terrific Ways
To Recruit Volunteers

Published by

Stevenson, Inc.
P.O. Box 4528 • Sioux City, Iowa • 51104
Phone 712.239.3010 • Fax 712.239.2166
www.stevensoninc.com

TABLE OF CONTENTS

TABLE OF CONTENTS

94 Terrific Ways to Recruit Volunteers — 2ⁿᵈ Edition

1. Job Descriptions Help Recruit the Right Volunteers

Want to find the right person to fill that specialized volunteer position? Rarely will the ideal candidate just walk through the door and offer to help. With the right effort, you can find a perfect match. Begin by looking at the whole picture. Create a comprehensive job description. Include the following:

- **Skills.** What skills and experience are necessary to accomplish the job?

- **Time requirements.** How many hours a week? How many months/years?

- **Travel considerations.** Is travel required? How will the volunteer be reimbursed?

- **Job description.** Detail all the responsibilities of the project, task or duty.

- **Timeline.** For this project, what are the markers and completion deadline?

- **Goals.** If the job requires fundraising, what amount are you trying to raise? If it is an event, who and how many are you targeting?

- **Resources.** Will the volunteer have access to agency phones, copy machines, office space and secretarial support; or is the work to be done independently from home?

- **Assistance.** Will others be recruited to assist? How many will be needed and what skills should they possess?

- **Reporting.** Who will train and advise the volunteer? Who will he/she report to?

- **Benefits.** It is human nature to participate because we get something from serving, be it personal empowerment, networking opportunities, individual growth or recognition.

2. Community Service Accomplishes Good, Attracts Volunteers

To recruit new volunteers, it may be necessary to attract some media coverage through community service projects.

By demonstrating that community service can be fun, build friendships and provide recognition for those who volunteer to be on your team, you also attract fresh faces and willing workers.

Think of projects that are sure to have significant value to the community, be newsworthy and encourage newcomers to jump on board with you. These techniques may help you get started:

- **Look for ways to fill needs in your community.** Almost every town and city has gaps in volunteer services. The elderly will always need help shopping, maintaining their homes and getting to doctors' appointments. At-risk teenagers often need after-school activities. The possibilities are endless when you can make a good match between your organization's mission and the needs of people who live in your service area.

- **Partner with another organization.** When a non-competing organization's services complement your own, meet with its staff to plan a joint activity where volunteers from both sides spend a day or weekend working together to meet a common goal for the good of the community. Volunteers from the other organization will become more familiar with yours, and vice versa. Cosponsor a childhood immunization effort or city-wide neighborhood watch crime prevention awareness month

with weekly programs and educational events. Spread efforts over a period of time to bring more opportunities for media coverage and more chances for volunteers to sign up.

- **Organize a community-wide volunteer fair.** Contact as many charitable organizations in your city as possible to see if they are interested based on your agency serving as the organizing catalyst. Ask for your mayor's support, create media kits and arrange for a site large enough for multiple organizations to set up recruitment booths and small displays about their volunteer opportunities. While your organization will be the primary sponsor and media contact, many others will benefit as well.

- **Ask a news organization to team with your philanthropic effort.** Television and radio stations frequently assist community organizations by airing public service announcements, sending a station personality to do remote broadcasts or telecasts from the scene and encouraging others to come out and sign up.

- **Get all the contact information you need.** Once you have planned an event that promises to attract new people to your organization, be sure to have several existing volunteers ready to take names and phone numbers. Have available brochures or flyers listing all volunteer jobs and including an interest indicator for would-be volunteers to complete. Encourage them to fill it out on the spot.

3. Step Up Recruitment Efforts When Demand Spikes

Just as more people than ever are relying on the critical services offered by many nonprofit organizations, you're probably also facing a need for more volunteers than ever to effectively manage that spike in demand.

This was the challenge faced at Dress for Success Oregon (Portland, OR), which promotes career development for unemployed women by providing them with career counseling services and free, professional attire, all provided by volunteers.

In 2009, Oregon's unemployment rate ranked second-highest in the nation; consequently, the Dress for Success organization saw demand increase threefold from 2008. How well did Dress for Success Oregon handle this demand? The chapter won the 2009 Nancy Lublin Founders Award, the highest honor given worldwide to Dress for Success organizations.

From a volunteer manager's perspective, how do you prepare for a significant uptick in demands for your services? Barbara Attridge, executive director of Dress for Success Oregon, outlines key steps:

1. **Track client numbers in a database,** allowing you to see fluctuations as soon as they occur.

2. **Keep a weekly schedule of appointment times to** which volunteers can commit. Attridge says Dress for Success Oregon was able to grow its volunteer force along with the increased demand. Appointments between clients and volunteer personal shoppers who help outfit them with new clothes run 60 to 90 minutes, Attridge says, so volunteers can commit to small, regularly occurring chunks of time rather than randomly scheduled, long stretches, making doing so convenient.

3. **Take advantage of media attention.** Attridge used all the media attention about unemployment as an opportunity to recruit volunteers as well as an outreach effort to attract more clients. In media interviews, she says, be sure and point out not only the services you provide, but the need for volunteers to help meet them.

4. **Realize that former clients can be your greatest resource.** When a person thanks you for helping him or her, that's the perfect time to pitch that person on giving back.

Source: Barbara Attridge, Executive Director, Dress for Success Oregon, Portland, OR. Phone (503) 249-7300.
E-mail: BarbaraA@dressforsuccessoregon.org.
Website: www.dressforsuccess.org/oregon

4. Low-tech Recruitment Method Brings in 500 Volunteers

Nearly 2,000 volunteers served at the Feed My Starving Children (Coon Rapids, MN) MobilePack™ food-packaging event, which took place Nov. 12-14, 2010.

Organized by 5th Bridge (Northfield, MN), a donor-focused organization whose mission is to enhance individual and community life in Northfield by encouraging the habits of volunteerism and philanthropy — the three-day volunteer event netted 534,600 meals for those in impoverished countries.

Organizers say a notably low-tech recruitment method helped draw a significant number of volunteers: placing clipboard sign-up sheets at local churches. Persons who signed up through this method numbered nearly 500, a full 25 percent of the total number of volunteers.

Candy Taylor, executive director of 5th Bridge, shares tips to maximize recruitment through clipboard placement:

- Place clipboards with sign-up sheets in the high-traffic areas of churches or other locations your target volunteer audience is likely to frequent.

- At the top of each sheet include name of the volunteer event, clearly defined dates of service, shift parameters and any information about attire or details needed for volunteering.

- Ask enrollees to provide names, phone numbers and e-mail addresses when signing up for a volunteer shift.

- Leave slips of paper or note cards by the sign-up sheet so volunteers can note the day and time they signed on to serve.

- Leave literature about the cause near the clipboard sign-up forms to answer participant questions along with a note or placard encouraging volunteers to take the brochure or information with them.

- Appoint a representative at the church to take charge of gathering clipboards and sending e-mail reminders that include details about the shift the volunteer signed on to complete to participants at least two days prior to the event.

Source: Candy Taylor, Executive Director, 5th Bridge, Northfield, MN. Phone (507) 581-3017. E-mail: candy@5thbridge.org.
Website: www.5thBridge.org

Recruitment Idea

Looking for early morning volunteers? Don't overlook evening shift workers who may be finishing their shifts at 7 a.m. or so. This is the equivalent of getting off of work at 5 p.m. for most people and their day is far from being over.

5. Offer Recently Widowed Individuals a Coping Alternative

Words cannot adequately describe what it's like to lose a spouse. It can be devastating and the grief can go on indefinitely.

Sometimes the best action the remaining spouse can take is to stay busy, perhaps taking on a new hobby or endeavor as a way to cope. That's where you come in. An invitation from you to the recently widowed individual may be just what the doctor ordered. Your gentle invitation asking the person to assist as a volunteer — at any level of involvement — may help the individual overcome some of the difficulties associated with the loss of a spouse. You will be doing the individual a service and, if he/she accepts your offer, you will be receiving service in return.

Develop a gentle letter such as the one shown here and send it to widowed individuals within a few weeks or months of their loss. You may be doing one another a favor.

Dear Mary:

I recognize that you and I don't know one another all that well, but you've been on my mind since the loss of your husband.

First, let me express my sympathy. I recognize that this must be a difficult time for you, and I hope that you are finding comfort through your family and friends. Please know my thoughts and prayers are with you.

Second, I want you to know that we would welcome your volunteer involvement here at St. Michael's whenever it works out for you. Sometimes getting involved in something new serves as one way of healing, particularly when that something new involves helping others. I just wanted to share that thought with you for your consideration.

Should you want to explore this further, please call me directly at 557-3221. Or, you can complete the enclosed card and return it to me, and I'll get back to you.

Sincerely,

Becky Elgin, Volunteer Services Director

---

6. Form Multiple Alliances to Assist With Multiple Projects

Why partner with one business or association when you could partner with several?

If you've ever partnered with a business, you know how much additional assistance can be provided for a particular project or program. Why not take that success to a new level by getting a number of businesses and other groups involved with your agency? To do that, first identify projects that could use volunteer assistance. List the number of volunteers required for each project or program along with general duties required to carry out each one. Once you've done that, identify a list of businesses and other types of groups — associations, clubs, churches/synagogues — that might make good partners. Then match projects/programs with appropriate groups. That way, when you approach each group, you will have a particular project in mind that best fits their group.

Below is an example of how one hospital attempted to identify projects/programs and match them with appropriate partners.

Partnership Opportunities — XYZ Hospital			
Project/Program	Potential Partner(s)	Volunteers Needed	Required Duties
St. Paddy's Fundraiser	St Michael's Knights of Columbus	30+	Mostly sell tickets and assist during event
Regular mailings, office help	RSVP Sr. Citizens Center	12-20	Fold, stuff, seal, etc. — appeals, newsletter, etc.
Annual phonathon	1st Financial Harker's Tingley University students	70	People willing to make calls over 5-night period
Speaker's bureau	Toastmasters	5+	Give presentations to local clubs, groups

7. Should You Form a Recruitment Committee?

Never seem to have enough volunteers? Assign recruitment tasks to a handful of volunteers whose sole purpose is to promote volunteer opportunities and enlist new volunteers.

Here's one method for accomplishing this:

A. Hand pick a group of existing volunteers to serve as ambassadors on behalf of your organization's volunteer efforts.

B. Give the group a name — Esprit de Corps, The (name of organization) Ambassadors, Volunteers-R-Us, etc. — and have members meet monthly.

C. Develop a committee description that defines the group's responsibilities. Allow members a hand in its development. Examples of ongoing responsibilities may include:

- Setting recruitment goals for the month, quarter and/or year.
- Inviting individuals to volunteer.
- Reviewing, approving and placing recruitment ads and literature.
- Speaking to groups about volunteer opportunities.
- Participating in and being present at volunteer job fairs.
- Coordinating volunteer-recruiting-volunteer campaigns.

With the assistance of this special committee, you should find recruitment efforts to be more focused and effective.

8. Implement Strategies That Reach Out to Minorities

If your organization is seeking to gain greater support from minorities in your area — whether it is their time, services or financial support — there are a number of points and possible approaches to consider before you start.

Begin by identifying the specific minority groups to whom you want to reach out. Do some of your programs and services benefit these people? Have any aspects of your mission changed to better serve their needs? If so, might they be willing and able to become volunteers when they no longer require assistance?

Try these strategies to enlist help from minority groups, which will build your organization's track record of successful programs that fill a variety of community needs:

- **Read publications produced by minority groups.** Depending on the size of your city, there may be many newspapers, magazines, newsletters or even television and radio programs that will help you become familiar with specific concerns or needs that may exist. Explore mutually beneficial relationships between members of your target minority group and your programs. Some may be looking for assistance, while others may desire a volunteer opportunity.

- **Seek out successful persons for their input.** Every group of individuals who share a cultural background has leaders and spokespersons, many of whom are successful in business or civic roles. Ask them to help your organization in long-range planning to better serve minority youth, families or seniors. If your goals and philosophies are compatible, they may consider acting as advisors, volunteers or board members.

- **Determine the varying degrees of needs.** As in every population, there will be persons who are successful and prosperous, middle income or in need of assistance. Seek a balance of involvement among them — those who can make contributions, those who can donate time and those who need your help. The success and experiences of those who are able to contribute can inspire those who are receiving and promote an atmosphere of dignity and cooperation for the entire organization.

- **Plan events that will be attractive to different cultures.** If your community has a significant population of a minority group, create festivals or other types of events that appeal to them. Ask minority leaders to help you with authenticity and accuracy — make the event a true celebration of diversity to appeal to all of your supporters.

- **Recognize the valuable perspective minorities can offer.** Remember that the world is getting smaller — we now speak of a global economy and overseas markets in business. The same applies to charitable organizations; if you are to grow and thrive, multicultural input will be essential to your growth and success.

9. Recruit Volunteers Through University Publications

Adding a college student to your volunteer corps has advantages beyond adding just an extra set of hands.

The Community Service Office at Washington University in St. Louis (St. Louis, MO) has been connecting college students with volunteer-driven community organizations since 1999. One way it does so is through the e-newsletter, The Community Service Connection, e-mailed to thousands of undergraduate and graduate students each week, which features announcements from community organizations looking for volunteers.

Stephanie Kurtzman, director of the university's community service office, says the newsletter is a way for organizations to recruit younger volunteers, which can be especially valuable for groups that work with teens and youth.

"Having a college student talk and work with these young people can make more of a positive impact on these youth than a person at a different stage of life," says Kurtzman. "It's also a way for organizations to find high-quality volunteers, since many of the students have professional skills they are excited to try out in areas such as marketing and graphic design."

The Newborns In Need Eastern Missouri Chapter (St. Louis, MO) used the e-newsletter to connect with student volunteers. Clem Roeder, chapter president, says the e-newsletter featured an ad seeking students with computer and marketing skills, volunteers to help with organizing donations, plus people to sew, knit and quilt items for the babies.

"We like students as volunteers mainly because they usually bring an inquisitive mind to the task, so we can spread the word as to the increasing need in our community," Roeder says.

To be featured in the e-newsletter, organizations submit information online or call the department. Kurtzman suggests posting information no more than three weeks in advance of the event. She also notes they do not repeat volunteer submissions, helping keep opportunities fresh.

Sources: Stephanie Kurtzman, Director, Community Service Office, Washington University in St. Louis, St. Louis, MO. Phone (314) 935-5066. E-mail: stephanie.kurtzman@wustl.edu. Website: http://communityservice.wustl.edu/csconnection/ Clem Roeder, President, Eastern Missouri Chapter of Newborns In Need, St. Louis, MO. Phone (314) 395-7582. E-mail: clemroeder@gmail.com

10. Illustrate What Can Be Achieved Based on Available Time

Can you think of times when even a half-hour contribution by a volunteer would be useful to your organization? Is the public aware of these short-term ways to help out?

One way to make people more aware of episodic volunteer opportunities is by developing a wish list of needs based on various time categories, then putting that list in brochures and other printed communications that the public can see.

This concept is illustrated in the example at right.

Recruitment Tip

Make it a rule: Never stand before a group of individuals without giving them an easy way to help your cause. Pass around a sign-up sheet, distribute a postcard they can mail back or get them involved in some other way; do more than extend an open-ended invitation to help.

We're Grateful For Whatever Time You Have to Give!

Here's a sampling of ways you can become involved — at your pace:

If you only have 30 minutes:
- ✓ Assist with a mailing.
- ✓ Run errands as needed.
- ✓ File.
- ✓ Help distribute mail.

If you have an hour:
- ✓ Answer phone/make phone calls.
- ✓ Organize supplies.
- ✓ Respond to website inquiries.

With two hours of volunteer time:
- ✓ Make some deliveries.
- ✓ Staff the front desk.
- ✓ Mentor a child.
- ✓ Give tours.

Half a day? Here's what you can do:
- ✓ Paint.
- ✓ Work in the gift shop.
- ✓ Help with our website.

We want and need your help. Whatever time you have available, whatever you enjoy doing, we're here to accommodate you.

Please give us a call at 555-4533 or stop by for more information.

11. Recruit and Manage Volunteers for Your Next Special Event

Recruiting special event volunteers allows your organization to plan events in an organized fashion with strong oversight. Officials with March of Dimes (Kalamazoo, MI) recruit special event volunteers to manage every detail of their events.

"The role of a special event volunteer is to serve the organization in a variety of capacities," says Dana DeLuca, March of Dimes division director. "Whether it be handling pre-event administrative tasks, serving as a committee member, cultivating event revenue or overseeing the event logistics, the special event volunteer is multi-faceted and plays an essential role in the overall success of an event. The most challenging task is finding the right role for each volunteer, managing to their strengths and giving them the tools to succeed and to feel successful."

DeLuca offers tips to recruit and manage special event volunteers:

❏ Make the ask. People can only respond if asked, and volunteer-minded persons are likely to offer something to your nonprofit. More often than not, says DeLuca, the volunteer with the most staying power has been asked to join the organization in a volunteer capacity to help move the mission forward.

❏ Determine the volunteer's specialty. Find what motivates each individual volunteer and assign him/her to opportunities according to those strengths. "It pays to find out what people are looking to gain from their role as volunteers and to help match them up with opportunities that best complement their desire to give back," says DeLuca.

❏ Give them the tools to succeed and get out of their way. Through the March of Dimes Volunteer Leadership Institute, an executive leadership program helps volunteers become experts in the organization. The program, DeLuca says, helps in recruiting and retaining strong board members, having successful events and providing effective programming. Tools offered to volunteers include educational items such as the publications shown at left that illustrate where gifts go and provide basic information about the March of Dimes so volunteers can speak in an informed way at special events.

Source: Dana DeLuca, Division Director, March of Dimes, Portage, MI. Phone (269) 343-5586. E-mail: ddeluca@marchofdimes.com. Website: www.marchofdimes.com/michigan

Content not available in this edition

Content not available in this edition

Content not available in this edition

Providing volunteers with educational items such as these helps prepare them to speak at special events on behalf of the March of Dimes (Portage, MI).

12. Make It Easy for Your Volunteers to Enlist Other Volunteers

Do you have a project coming up that will require two to three times the number of volunteers you presently have on hand? If so, here's a way to double or triple the number of willing participants for that special undertaking.

With a little up-front help on your part, your existing volunteers can appeal to friends, associates and family members to boost numbers for your upcoming project.

Supply each volunteer with a packet of five note cards with a preprinted message (see example at right) and coordinating envelopes. Ask each one to add a handwritten salutation at the beginning of the message, sign the notes (adding a P.S. if they wish), and address the envelopes to five individuals they think would make good volunteer prospects for this onetime project. Then have them enclose the note cards, seal the envelopes, stamp them and drop them in the mail. It's as simple as that!

After two or three days have gone by — enough time for the recipients to have gotten their invitations — instruct the volunteers to phone each of their five contacts as an enlistment follow-up. Have the volunteers phone your office (or complete a return postcard that went out with the

---

(Salutation and Name)

I could sure use three hours of your help for a onetime project I'm working on.

As you know, I'm a regular volunteer for the West High School Boosters. On Saturday, March 22, we're hosting about 50 area high school band members (and many of their parents), who will be participating in a music contest here. It's a great opportunity for our Booster Association to raise needed funds for special improvements to West High.

Even though it's an all-day event, I'd really appreciate it if you could give just three hours of your time to help us out. You can either choose how you want to help or have a job assigned to you.

I'll be phoning you in the next few days to check your availability for this project.

Thank you so much for giving my request your positive consideration!

(Name and P.S.)

---

original mailing to them) to report on who agreed to help. Get the new volunteers' addresses, phone numbers and e-mail addresses so your office can take it from there.

Even if you only get a 20 percent response rate, that's one new volunteer from every group of five note cards sent out. And, if every existing volunteer sent out a packet of five, you will have doubled the number of existing volunteers.

13. Create No Frills Training, Opportunities for Busy Volunteers

In today's on-the-go society, time is tight for many people. Their jobs demand most of their attention; they're working and raising families; they're multitasking throughout their day; often, they are very driven personalities.

Yet, many such people may be willing to volunteer if able to do so on their own time and terms.

How can you accommodate these individuals who want to make a meaningful contribution and then get on with their lives? How can you convince them that you will meet them on their terms? Try these proven methods:

- Develop a menu of specific tasks from which they can choose that include brief job descriptions and the time estimated to complete each duty.

- Avoid offering volunteer jobs in which outside factors — setting appointments with others, tasks that involve waiting — may impede the timely completion of their responsibilities.

- Eliminate any frills — socializing, waiting for others to arrive, etc. — that prevents these volunteers from starting and finishing projects on their time.

- Keep training time to the point and as brief as possible. Consider sending training material in advance to avoid using on-the-job time for that purpose.

- Provide them with multiple choices of times in which to show up and complete tasks.

- Err on the side of protecting their time. If, for instance, a task has not yet been fully completed by the time the volunteer said he/she would need to leave, have another volunteer prepared to step in and complete it for him/her.

Chances are good that you can keep these no-frills volunteers coming back if you can accommodate their demands early on in your relationship with them. Although each volunteer commitment may be a brief in-and-out experience — or even involve their working from home — they will come to claim your organization as their own in time.

14. Identify and Welcome Your Community's Newcomers

Why shouldn't your organization be among the first to welcome newcomers to your community and, while you're at it, extend an invitation to get involved as volunteers? Giving newcomers an opportunity to volunteer provides them with a quick-start method of meeting others and learning the ins and outs of their new community.

Here's how to get a newcomers' program up and running:

1. **Establish contacts through first-to-know professionals** — realtors, bankers, etc. — so your organization can be notified whenever someone new has moved into the community.

2. **Assemble baskets of goodies to be distributed to newcomers.** In addition to literature about your own organization and volunteer opportunities, include other useful resources: chamber of commerce directory, listing of all community nonprofits, religious organizations, etc. Get businesses to donate useful items or coupons as gift items as well.

3. **Assemble a group of volunteers to serve as welcome hosts,** delivering the welcome baskets to newcomers and inviting them to consider volunteer opportunities.

4. **Once a quarter (or twice each year), host a reception for all newcomers at your facility.** Use the event to make introductions and offer tours of your agency. Invite local public officials to be present to welcome the newcomers as well.

15. Develop Plan to Attract Single Volunteers

Single Volunteers of Northeast Ohio (Cleveland, OH) offers a simple approach to volunteerism for singles in the region by offering free membership. The organization is a social membership offering area singles the ability to meet while supporting various community groups through volunteering.

"Because we have one thing in common, being single, it benefits our members as we immediately all have something in common," says Debbie Kean, president.

If you are seeking to grow your volunteer numbers, learn from the successes of Volunteer Singles. Kean shares strategies that have made Single Volunteers of Northeast Ohio one of the most sought after membership organizations by singles:

❏ *Make members feel comfortable and welcome at all events, particularly meetings.* If new members or volunteers have fun at an event and — if they have been made to feel comfortable — they will be telling friends about Single Volunteers. Follow these ways to encourage socializing and fun at meetings:

• Engage attendees in ice-breaker games.

• Assign greeters at each meeting to sign in attendees as they enter the meeting. Greeters also shake hands and tell about the group.

• Enlist officers to go from table to table during the meeting, introducing themselves to new attendees.

❏ *Offer volunteer activities and events that naturally attract singles.* While service is the key to this organization, social gatherings are also promoted at the nonprofit's website. Under the Cleveland Events tab of the website, one can find mention of summer dances and rib cook-offs intermingled with volunteer events. The blend makes it easy for singles to mix and mingle as well as lend a hand.

❏ *Involve board members.* At monthly meetings board members are asked to sit at a different table, which allows all new attendees to have an opportunity to ask questions about the membership group. These board members are also the biggest advocates of the group and are not shy about talking-up Single Volunteers.

❏ *Assign a social greeter.* Single Volunteers also assigns a point of contact at each event whose job it is to coordinate the event as well as to make each person feel welcome.

❏ *Heavily promote the organization's website and purpose.* This organization's website at www.svohio. org is advertised in local newspapers, as well as social networks, and receives feedback that those publications are, in fact, getting the word out.

Source: Debbie Kean, President, Singles Volunteers of Northeast Ohio, Olmsted Falls, OH. Phone (216) 534-7024. E-mail: singlevolunteers.cleveland@yahoo.com. Website: www.svohio.org

Recruitment Tip

If your nonprofit is based in a small community or rural area, try collaborating with other nonprofits to formulate joint recruiting strategies. You may find that individuals are willing to divide their time among multiple organizations

16. Recruiting From New Pool of Volunteers

Looking for fresh ways to tap previously untapped volunteer sources? Here are five ideas to get you started:

1. **Create an interactive volunteer web page** where anyone who accesses your website can fill out an application online and/or e-mail questions about volunteer opportunities. Make sure your agency's home page has an easy-to-find link to this page.

2. **Recruit through churches** by first setting up an easy, fun program to get congregation members through the door.

3. **Participate in school and university programs that require community service hours** and recruit those participants to come back as volunteers.

4. **Go to the people who have benefited from your organization;** when and where appropriate to do so, recruit clients and their family members.

5. **Create an award system for volunteers who recruit other volunteers.** Make it a fun competition with donated door prizes.

17. Fashion Attractor Projects for Entry-level Volunteers

Do you have a menu of tasks and projects for new volunteers who want to help but are still unsure of how much time to commit and what to do?

Your odds of building a long-term relationship with volunteers will increase if you are careful about easing them into the process. Some ways to do so:

- Develop a list of specific tasks from which volunteers may choose.

- Limit the time to complete those tasks to two hours.

- Include a sheet of printed instructions for each of the entry-level tasks.

- Explain how the completion of each task fits into your organization's big picture. What will the task's completion help to accomplish?

- Select tasks that offer flexibility as to the time or day of the week they get completed.

- Offer both group and individual tasks.

- Include projects that can be completed at the volunteer's home or office.

- Share the name of a staff person (or veteran volunteer) to whom the new recruit can turn to for help.

18. Tap Volunteers for Co-worker Connections

Need more volunteers? Take a closer look at your existing volunteer pool for ideas on where — and whom — to recruit.

Have recent retirees? Ask them about their former place of employment. Do they know of soon-to-be retired persons or part-timers willing to join them as volunteers?

Have high schoolers? Ask if they have part-time jobs. If so, would they be willing to ask if other co-workers would have spare time to give your organization?

Finally, touch base with episodic or special event volunteers who may have full-time obligations and can only offer their time to your organization on special occasions. Do they know of others in similar situations who could come along next time?

Be ready to provide these important contacts with one-page volunteer recruitment flyers or business cards to post or share at their former or current place of work.

Then look for visible ways to recognize volunteers who bring in new recruits.

19. Invite the Self-employed To Join Your Ranks

The number of self-employed people in this country is growing. Why not tap into that trend by recruiting self-employed individuals to volunteer for your organization?

Self-employed people tend to be highly motivated. They have an entrepreneurial spirit and are often eager to share their expertise. They also know that volunteering can be an excellent way to network with potential clients.

Don't know how to approach the self-employed about volunteering? Just ask them. Invite the person to lunch and outline what he or she can do for your organization. You might just be surprised by the person's willingness to help.

20. Find Volunteers to Serve at Special Events

Volunteers can help make your special event a brilliant success. However, finding the right volunteers for your event can be the critical key to planning and pulling off a flawless event. Look in these places to find the right volunteers for your event:

- *Trade schools or universities* — Post notices on secondary school websites for short-term internships for interested students to help plan your event. Students studying mass communications, marketing or other related fields of study will be interested in getting their feet wet in the real world.

- *Alternative schools* — Look to alternative high school students proficient in art or music to provide those skills at your event. Talented and gifted students often attend these schools and would most likely be happy to participate in your event.

- *Culinary students* — Seek out culinary schools to find students interested in showcasing their talents at your event. Ask for a team of students to prepare a portion of the meal, such as dessert, at your event.

- *Interns* — Search for those performing internships at local businesses. Those working in marketing or event planning internships will be well-suited to assisting in planning your event and doing so will give them an additional credit to their resume.

21. Brochure Points Out How Businesses Can Help

You probably have a brochure designed to help recruit individual volunteers, but what about a brochure that reaches out specifically to area businesses?

To make the most of forming new partnerships and making businesses aware of volunteer opportunities and ways to support your volunteer programs, design a brochure that's tailored specifically to them. (See the example below and at right.) You can send the brochure along with a letter of invitation, or leave it with individual business contacts following one-on-one visits. The brochures could also be distributed at various gatherings where business representatives are present.

Many businesses may simply be unaware of how they can become involved with your organization. A printed piece such as this can be used to help build your case and list the many ways in which businesses can support your efforts — as sponsors, providing volunteer assistance through their employees, hosting events on your behalf, mentoring and much more.

And don't forget to include copy that points out the direct benefits to businesses (e.g., enhanced image within the community/region, etc.).

Partner With Us!

There are so many ways in which your business could assist our efforts. Here are but a few:

- ❑ Allow your employees to volunteer time during their working hours.
- ❑ Sponsor one of our many volunteer-driven events.
- ❑ Become involved in the committee of your choice.
- ❑ Allow us to host an event at your facility.
- ❑ Encourage your employees to become volunteers.
- ❑ Underwrite the cost of a new program.
- ❑ Serve as mentors.
- ❑ Allow us to give a program to your employees.
- ❑ Explore a profit-sharing campaign with one of your products. (X percent of all sales — during this period of time — will go to this agency.)
- ❑ Offer to join our board of directors.
- ❑ Collaborate with us on a community betterment project.
- ❑ Explore ways in which your company's equipment, expertise or products might be used to offset our agency's expenses (e.g., printing our publications, conducting a survey, making your product/service free for our agency).

Consider This Your Invitation....

We take this opportunity to invite you to partner with us and welcome whatever level of participation you choose.

You will find a partnership to be mutually beneficial. A few of the business perks you will receive include:

- ✓ Publicity about deeds you have completed through or on behalf of our agency.
- ✓ Various training opportunities for any of your employees who choose to volunteer for us.
- ✓ Reduced rate access for your employee volunteers to our facility.
- ✓ Free tickets to events for any of your employee volunteers.

And the list goes on....

22. Pointers for Recruiting Volunteers to Assist Children, Parents

At Yale-New Haven Hospital (YNHH) of New Haven, CT, volunteers are key to The Bright Beginnings Family Read Program, which brings together first-time parents and their children for reading and positive parenting through selected children's books.

The program offers free transportation, a light meal and on-site child care, which is provided by volunteers.

Melissa Rowe, program manager, shares tips for recruiting volunteers to work with children:

- Send flyers into the community and network with agencies, private childcare providers and within your nonprofit.

- Encourage staff and board members to refer potential volunteers through word-of-mouth, church groups and other community organizations.

- Design a recruitment brochure. YNHH has a recruitment brochure to recruit volunteers for three programs, one of which is Family Read.

- Enlist the help of your parent advisory board. YNHH has a dedicated recruitment committee whose members visit colleges and other community venues with presentations about the program.

- Ask members of your parent advisory board to volunteer for the program.

- Expand your volunteer base. YNHH's department of volunteer services, under the direction of Jeannette Hodge, funnels volunteers to the Family Read program based on the expressed interest of the volunteer to work with children and parents.

- Have a website presence. The YNHH website includes the Family Read program under the Volunteer Opportunities section of the website.

Source: Melissa Rowe, Program Manager, Department of Social Work, Yale-New Haven Hospital, New Haven, CT. Phone (203) 688-5996. E-mail: Melissa.Rowe@ynhh.org. Website: www.ynhh.org

23. Volunteering Provides Strong Reminder for Military Families

What started as a coffee group of persons whose loved ones — members of the Headquarters and Headquarters Company 1st Brigade Combat Team stationed at Ft. Stewart, GA — were serving in Iraq soon grew to much more.

The group members decided to move beyond simply meeting for coffee to do something positive for the local community. So they volunteered to make dinner for families staying at the local Ronald McDonald House.

Anna Burns, a member of the group and volunteer with Ronald McDonald House Charities of the Coastal Empire (Savannah, GA), says volunteering was a way for them to connect with the local community that ended up hitting close to home.

"We were most surprised to hear about families from the military community who are served by the (Ronald McDonald) house when their children are being treated at the local hospitals," Burns says. "We were helping out other families in Savannah and also those in our own community and situation."

The experience also taught the volunteers about various programs they could take back to the Ft. Stewart community to continue helping the nonprofit, such as collecting pop tabs or donations for cleaning supplies.

But, Burns says, perhaps the most important benefit for the military volunteers was the opportunity to remind themselves that everyone makes sacrifices and that everyone goes through tough times. "Through caring for one another, we can all heal with love and support. One kind gesture could change someone's day, and not worrying about your next meal while you have a sick child to care for is a kindness that cannot be replaced."

Source: Anna Burns, Account Executive, Dalton Agency, Savannah, GA. Phone (904) 881-6107. E-mail: aburns@daltonagency.com

Get Military Families Involved

Want to get military families involved in volunteering at your organization? Just ask, says Anna Burns, a member of a local military group and also a Ronald McDonald House Charities of the Coastal Empire (Savannah, GA) volunteer.

"The best way to contact them is through the Family Readiness Support Assistant (FRSA) program," she says. "The FRSAs are civil servants contracted by the military post who serve as a critical link between the command team and local community. The FRSA can reach out to the Family Readiness Groups (FRG). From there it can trickle down to other unaffiliated groups who just want to support a good cause."

24. Attract Young Adult Volunteers

The 20-something crowd can be a valuable demographic, both for the energy young people can bring to your organization today, and for the longevity they can bring to your organization over their lifetimes.

Levé (Portland, OR) is a six-year-old nonprofit with a mission to support other local charitable organizations through fundraising and board building. Every Levé board member and volunteer is under 29 years old, says Kiernan Doherty, vice president. "We're always at full capacity and replenishing our board with new members."

To boost volunteer participation by the under-30 crowd, Doherty recommends:

1. **Align your thinking with your volunteers' values.** "We're much more entrepreneurial," says Doherty of herself and her peers. "We want to take a lot of ownership in our activities and want more autonomy." She suggests always asking a young adult to donate time as well as money to make the person feel more empowered and more a part of things than just signing a check. Once you establish a trusting relationship with younger participants, encourage them to come up with ideas for fundraisers. They will likely want to run the show themselves, which means more money and less work for you.

2. **Create an ambassador board.** Doherty has seen more ambassador boards showing up as an inventive way to engage 20- and 30-somethings. Charge this junior board of directors with planning one major fundraiser a year that caters to an under-35 audience.

3. **Ask people to party for your nonprofit!** Doherty says every Levé fundraiser has one thing in common: fun! The best way to introduce your organization to a young adult is to invite him or her to a party in honor of it — ideally with a low ticket price and with drink sales going to your coffers as well. "When people come to our events, they see 15 board members having fun, and they see the collective impact of everyone giving their time and money," says Doherty. "It's a great advertisement for what we do."

Source: Kiernan Doherty, Vice President, Levé, Portland, OR. Phone (503) 320-7076. E-mail: kdoherty@metgroup.com

25. Maximize Your Volunteer Program by Enlisting the Very Best

When you learn of persons whom you believe would make ideal volunteer leaders, develop a plan to enlist them. Follow these steps to go about recruiting top candidates:

✓ **Answer "yes" questions.** Before approaching a candidate, first ask why he/she would say "yes" to your invitation to volunteer. Doing so will point out the need for adequate background information on the candidate and help shape your presentation.

✓ **Develop an appointment plan.** Who should set the appointment? Who should attend? Stack the deck in your favor in order to avoid a negative response.

✓ **Make the request compelling.** By doing your homework, you will sense what motivates the candidate to say "yes" to your request. A critical cause? Corporate or personal visibility? Association with other prominent individuals? Point out the perceived benefits of serving your cause.

✓ **Describe the big picture and the value of top volunteer leadership within it.** What will the project consist of, start to finish? What is the time frame? Define how appropriate leadership will make a positive impact in your project's eventual success.

✓ **Be clear in your expectations.** Will the position require significant time on the volunteer's part? Will it require enlisting other individuals? If you expect the candidate to follow through on expectations, share these expectations in advance.

Recruitment Idea

To build your corps of volunteers, send an e-mail or postcard to a random sampling of your community with the following message: "Could you give just one hour of your time during the week of (insert dates)? If you can, please call (insert phone number) to schedule an hour that works best for you." Since you are only asking for one hour, you may be surprised at how many will participate. It's worth testing.

26. Three Ways to Recruit Volunteers Online

Have you ever considered using the web to recruit volunteers? Following is a list of ways to utilize the Internet to increase your volunteer numbers.

1. **Use an online opportunities list.** Do you include a detailed position description? The more information you can give the better. Attention spans are short; give the surfer as much information as possible, right from the beginning. Also include your e-mail address or create a separate e-mail address just for online recruitment so your current inbox doesn't get overloaded. Most volunteer opportunity lists are free, so put opportunities on multiple sites.

2. **Make sure your website is recruitment friendly.** Put a visible link, like a highlighted box, to your volunteer page on every page of your website, home, other departments, etc. Beyond that have the link list available, volunteer opportunities and an online application. Make signing up to volunteer online as easy as possible.

3. **Create a newsgroup.** A newsgroup is like an online community where its members can chat, receive notices, etc. You can create your own site for your volunteers and direct prospective volunteers to it. Newsgroups can also be searched based on topic. Check out groups.google.com for an online tour and instructions to set up your own group.

Volunteer Opportunities Websites

Some websites dedicated to volunteering include:

Network for Good — www.networkforgood.org

VolunteerMatch — www.volunteermatch.org

Craig's List — www.craigslist.org

1-800 Volunteer — www.1-800-volunteer.org

Monster.com — www.volunteer.monster.com

Idealist — www.idealist.org

Volunteer Solutions — www.volunteersolutions.org

National Mentoring Partnership — www.mentor.org

---

27. Ideas to Engage Volunteers in Changing Economic Times

Following a 2010 survey of volunteers and nonprofit leaders in the state, the Minnesota Association for Volunteer Administration (MAVA), Maplewood, MN, released tips for seeking and engaging volunteers in the changing economic times, including:

- Customize involvement to fit the volunteer's interests, talents and availability. Give volunteers opportunities to describe how they would like to help and then work with them to create new volunteer opportunities.

- Be flexible in response to the schedule and requirements of the volunteer. ... Offer more short-term or episodic, weekend and evening volunteer opportunities.

- Find ways to engage volunteers during nonworking hours, for one-time or short-term projects and events.

- Offer expanded roles for volunteers in the organization. Encourage volunteers to assist with the development or enhancement of new roles.

- Offer opportunities to lead projects. Send the message that this is a community initiative and volunteering offers stakeholders a role in the development of the project by creating meaningful projects that are highly flexible.

- Provide volunteer opportunities that use professional skills and have higher levels of responsibility.

- Involve volunteers in recruiting other volunteers.

- Connect with colleges and schools in your area and offer classroom presentations to engage students in the area.

- Increase use of technology in recruiting and communicating with volunteers by way of Twitter and Facebook.

- Form partnerships to recruit volunteers and to work on projects of joint interest with like-minded nonprofits.

- Market volunteer positions to job seekers and support them to get the most out of the experience. Stress the fact that continued involvement in their community enhances rèsumès. Promote volunteering as a way to gain experience in a field where employment is desired.

Source: Mary Quirk, Volunteer Resources Leadership Project Manager, Minnesota Association for Volunteer Administration, Maplewood, MN. Phone (651) 255-0469. E-mail: mquirk@mavanetwork.org. Website: www.mavanetwork.org

28. Regularly Host and Attend Volunteer Fairs

Don't let the thought of organizing a volunteer fair overwhelm you, says James Leary, vice chancellor of community and government relations at the University of Massachusetts Medical School (UMASS), Worcester, MA. The process "is a lot easier to do than you think, and the rewards are tremendous, both for your employees and for the community."

UMASS hosts an annual volunteer fair that draws hundreds of attendees. As a large medical school, UMASS has a public service mission at its core, says Leary, and a volunteer fair connects employees, faculty and students with volunteer opportunities.

"We enable them to learn about these opportunities and apply their individual skills to address the entire spectrum of community need, from health care to education, hunger initiatives to youth development, homelessness to the environment," says Leary.

John Craven, volunteer and construction coordinator for Habitat for Humanity (Worcester, MA), represents one of almost 30 organizations that attend UMASS's volunteer fair. The event, he says, "gives our organization the opportunity to spread the word about the local Habitat for Humanity affiliate in a different venue."

The Donald W. Reynolds Library (Mountain Home, AR) also hosts a volunteer fair every year. "Many people really would like to volunteer, but don't," says Kim Crow Sheaner, community outreach coordinator. "A volunteer fair helps them by creating a very non-threatening environment where they can visit with organizations and find the best fit for their interests and talents. Meanwhile, the organizations benefit because they get to visit with a concentrated group of people who have a sincere interest in volunteering."

So what does it take to have a successful fair? Both Crow Sheaner and Leary agree that partnerships are key.

"When we started ours five years ago, we asked the chamber of commerce to co-sponsor the event," says Crow Sheaner. "They assist with the planning and set-up. We also added a local radio station and newspaper as sponsors in exchange for advertising. Another sponsor, a local grocery store, provides a sack lunch for each of the organizations, so the representatives do not have to leave their booths during the fair."

The volunteer fair experts share ways to spread the word about your volunteer fair:

- Send messages through social media venues, including Facebook and Twitter.
- Place ads and news articles in your local newspaper.
- Ask your local radio and TV stations to produce public service announcements.
- Seek interviews with the event organizer or a key volunteer on local radio and TV.
- Send e-mails to everyone in your e-mail database.
- Place posters throughout your community.
- Feature the event within your organization, through hardcopy and online publications, your website, banners, in-house TV monitors and elsewhere.
- Promote the event through your local chamber of commerce.

Sources: John Craven, Volunteer and Construction Coordinator, AmeriCorps*VISTA Habitat for Humanity — MetroWest/Greater Worcester, Worcester, MA. Phone (508) 799-9259, ext. 113. E-mail: John.Craven@habitatmwgw.org. Website: www.habitatmwgw.org
Kim Crow Sheaner, Community Outreach Coordinator, Donald W. Reynolds Library, Mountain Home, AR. Phone (870) 580-0987, ext. 2143. E-mail: kim.c@baxtercountylibrary.org
James Leary, Vice Chancellor of Community and Government Relations, University of Massachusetts Medical School, Worcester, MA. Phone (508) 856-2000. E-mail: James.Leary@umassmed.edu

---

Set Your Organization Apart At Volunteer Fairs

If you decide to attend a volunteer fair organized by another community group, how do you set your organization apart from the rest?

Paulette Hill, mentor coordinator for Baxter County Juvenile Services (Mountain Home, AR), regularly participates in a volunteer fair at the Donald W. Reynolds Library (Mountain Home, AR).

To set your organization apart, Hill suggests you:

- ❑ Set up your booth or table close to the entrance.
- ❑ If your organization works with children and youth, schedule some of these young people to help at your booth to put a face with the program and attract potential volunteers of all ages.
- ❑ Be engaged. Stand up and walk around to other booths.
- ❑ Have brochures/pamphlets for people to take home.
- ❑ Network with other organizations. Many people volunteer at more than one organization, so work with other groups to share the volunteers.
- ❑ Encourage potential volunteers to fill out an interest card. Keep it simple. Ask for name, e-mail address and phone numbers. This allows you to follow up with people interested in volunteering at your organization.

Since most material she uses already exists, preparing for a volunteer fair takes Hill just a few hours. "It's worth all the time you spend on it," she says. "Unlike a presentation at a Lions Club or Rotary, a volunteer fair is an audience filled with people who are serious about volunteering."

Source: Paulette Hill, Mentor Coordinator, Baxter County Juvenile Services, Mountain Home, AR. Phone (870) 421-2604. E-mail: phill@bcjs.org.

29. Ask Your Newspaper to Include a Work Wanted Section

It's common for many newspapers to devote space to a Volunteers Needed section on a regular basis, but here's another twist: Why not convince the newspaper to include a Volunteer Work Wanted section — perhaps on a monthly basis — to test what might result from it? The newspaper may even agree to running the work wanted ads at no cost to the persons submitting the listing.

If all area volunteer agencies approached the newspaper to try the concept for a year, it might help in matching willing volunteers with the most appropriate jobs. In addition, the volunteer work wanted ads might spur others in the community to get involved with service as well.

Volunteer Work Wanted Classifieds

40-something communications executive willing to contribute to or possibly serve as editor for a nonprofit agency's newsletter.

Willing and able homemaker, and mother of three, willing to do work from my home one afternoon a week.

Recently retired high school teacher wants the opportunity to work with youth two afternoons a week.

Retired 63-year-old man willing to do limited handyman jobs for agency needing help.

Female high school junior would like to give one or two hours of service after school three days a week. Preferably some people-to-people responsibilities.

8-to-5 working female willing to take on limited work from my home in the evenings — signing, assembling, collating, etc.

Male university sophomore majoring in computer science hoping to find intern position. Will set up or expand agency's website.

Corporate executive willing to facilitate day-long nonprofit planning retreat.

55-year-old Spanish-speaking female willing to serve as mentor. Available 4 hours per week.

30. Recruit and Support Volunteer Interpreters

As communities grow in diversity, so does the value of volunteer interpreters.

At the Volunteer Interpreter Program at the Fairfax County Juvenile and Domestic Relations District Court (JDRDC) in Fairfax, VA, the need for volunteer interpreters has increased every year since its 1994 founding, says Coordinator Loida Gibbs.

Forty interpreters currently volunteer with the program, each working an average of one four-hour shift a week to assist juvenile courthouse staff and families who come through the court system, Gibbs says.

The demand for Spanish interpreters is the highest, while the court also has translators for Portuguese, French, Quechua and Italian, the coordinator says. Gibbs says if someone who speaks a language other than these needs assistance, staff can call Language Line Services (Monterey, CA), which offers interpreters for 170 languages.

When it comes to recruiting volunteers who speak another language, Gibbs says current volunteers are your best resource. "What works best for this program is word of mouth by the volunteers themselves," she says. "We do advertise online and with local volunteer agencies, as well as using newspaper write-ups. Since I speak the language, it's easy for me to find the volunteers. Networking is very important in this field."

Working in a courtroom setting, these interpreters undergo mandatory training sessions to ensure they understand their role, including court procedures, justice system concepts and terminology, confidentiality, ethics and courtroom demeanor.

Since volunteer interpreters have specialized skills, Gibbs says it's important to encourage the volunteers to stay up-to-date with the latest news about interpreters. "Many of the interpreters are members of the National Association of Judiciary Interpreters and Translators as well as the American Translators Association. Some of them, of their own initiative, attend conferences (and) workshops to better themselves in this field."

In addition to interpreter conferences and workshops, Gibbs stresses the importance of having a personal relationship with these men and women.

"We have get-togethers throughout the year for all the volunteers and their families," the volunteer coordinator says. "During those potluck events I like to make a big deal in front of their families and let them know how much they do and what they do for the courthouse." Plus, she says, these get-togethers allow her to learn interpreters' needs, such as if they are in need of more training, and if so, what kind.

Sources: Loida Gibbs, Volunteer Interpreter Program Coordinator, Fairfax County Juvenile & Domestic Relations District Court, Fairfax, VA. Phone (703) 246-7581. E-mail: Loida.Gibbs@ fairfaxcounty.gov. Website: www.fairfaxcounty.gov/courts/jdr

31. Seek and Assign Volunteers With Writing Skills

Identifying volunteers with specific skills can offer your organization the opportunity to tap those skills for the betterment of your nonprofit.

Beth Upham, manager of volunteer services at the Morristown Memorial Hospital (Morristown, NJ), has identified three volunteers with keen writing and interviewing abilities and has focused their efforts on one specific project. These volunteers have been assigned to interview fellow Depression era volunteers to capture their stories by recording their memories and service at the hospital.

Upham uses the information to feature volunteers in her newsletter. She has also created posters featuring the Depression era volunteers and their interviews, sharing them at the annual volunteer luncheon and on the organization's website.

To manage a volunteer writing project and utilize the final interviews, Upham recommends:

- Obtaining permission from the volunteers who will be interviewed.
- Giving the volunteer writer contact information for the volunteer story subjects.
- Working with the volunteer writer to establish a deadline for his/her story.
- Offering the volunteer writer full credit for all published work as a benefit for working on the project.
- Sharing the published stories with staff. Hospital staff is always interested in learning more about the volunteers they interact with and see in the hallways.

Source: Beth Upham, Manager of Volunteer Services and Pastoral Care, Morristown Memorial Hospital, Morristown, NJ. Phone (973) 971-5476. E-mail: Beth.Upham@atlantichealth.org. Website: www.morristownmemorialhospital.org

32. Top 10 List Emphasizes Volunteer Needs

Staff at the Red Door Animal Shelter (Chicago, IL) use a Top 10 list of volunteer opportunities as a simple yet effective way to express their current volunteer needs.

At the Red Door website, volunteers can easily locate the organization's top 10 critical needs from volunteers. The importance of this Top 10 list for Red Door includes help with laundry, driving, shelter shopping, animal caretaking, foster homes, veterinary technicians, phone calls, adoptions, special events and special projects.

"It was important for us to highlight our volunteer needs because both volunteers and prospective volunteers like to know what opportunities they can choose to make a difference with our organization," says Matt Gannon, manager of the animal shelter.

"So, even if someone says 'I'm not really a cat person (or dog person, etc.),' that person can look at the list of needs and say, 'but, I would be more than willing to help with transporting animals, or come in and do laundry or some other listed task for a day.'"

Gannon says volunteers enjoy having the list to refer to from time to time. "As an organization, we leave it up to volunteers to decide the areas and ways that they are comfortable helping out with. Some volunteers only do socialization with animals, some only help with fundraising and events. This way, volunteers can define specialties they excel in, as opposed to being assigned volunteer work they may not feel comfortable doing."

He says the list has helped with recruitment because it allows prospective volunteers to stop by and say, "What do you need from me?" It helps with retention, he says, as some volunteers who may be feeling some burnout from working in one particular area can find other ways to support the shelter.

Check out the animal shelter's list of top 10 volunteer needs at: http://www.reddoorshelter.org/volunteer-needs.html

Source: Matt Gannon, Manager, Red Door Animal Shelter, Chicago, IL. Phone (773) 764-2242. E-mail: mgannon@reddoorshelter.org. Website: www.reddoorshelter.org

Recruitment Idea

Here's a fun way to get the word out on your highest priority needs: Create and advertise your 10 Most Wanted list. It makes a great way to let the public know what some of your needs are in an attention-getting way.

Advertise for key volunteer positions, equipment, supplies and more. To add another level of fun, offer a reward — dead or alive — to those persons who supply your requests.

33. Engage Volunteers Who Can Share Their Skills, Talents

Consider enlisting highly skilled persons to promote the mission of your organization.

Volunteers with Arts in Prison (AiP) of Overland Park, KS, work to facilitate personal growth of local inmates through 10- to 12-week courses in fine arts.

Volunteers — including professional artists, retired teachers and art students — share their passion for music, painting, ceramics, sculpture, speech, drama, creative writing, yoga, photography and gardening. Working with AiP staff, the volunteers select the type of class they wish to present and develop it to their specifications.

Leigh Lynch, associate director of AiP, offers the following steps for volunteers working on class development:

- **Undergo volunteer training**. Even though these volunteers will be teaching others, they still need to complete volunteer training to learn about your organization. At AiP, teaching volunteers undergo volunteer training through the nonprofit and the prison institution where they will offer classes to learn rules and expectations.

- **Issue statement of intent**. Require new volunteers to prepare a statement of intent outlining the structure of the course and curriculum involved, as well as how the course will align with the missions of your program.

- **Set class time, length.** Have staff work with volunteers to determine class times, term and length based on the curriculum outlined in the statement of intent.

- **Decide location.** Determine where the class will be held. If offsite, work with the hosting venue to schedule the class.

- **Define class size.** Work with the teaching volunteer to determine appropriate class size based on the nature of the class and the comfort level of the teaching volunteer.

- **Support.** Consider the need for a teaching assistant or an additional volunteer who can help expedite the class.

- **Observe**. Require that new volunteers developing their own classes observe a current class and teaching techniques. Additionally, have staff observe new volunteers in order to provide supportive feedback.

- **Require a break period.** Teaching can take its toll. Require that teaching volunteers take a breather between teaching semesters to become refreshed and rejuvenated. At AiP, volunteer instructors are encouraged to take two weeks off between class semesters.

Source: Leigh Lynch, Associate Director, Arts in Prison, Overland Park, KS. Phone (913) 403-0229. E-mail: leighl@artsinprison.org. Website: www.artsinprison.org

34. Share Your Story to Celebrate Volunteers, Entice Newcomers

Share your organization's story to draw the attention of potential volunteers, donors and members while helping your current volunteers realize the caliber of the organization for which they volunteer.

Create a dedicated spot on your website for special volunteer stories. Then use these ideas to gather compelling stories:

- Ask volunteers or clients who have a heartwarming story about your nonprofit to share that story with the community through an article in the local newspaper, by telling it on the radio or television news or by sharing it in your newsletter.

- Watch for nationally recognized celebrations that have connections to your nonprofit's mission (e.g., National Older Americans Month in May or National Hunger Awareness Month in June). As that month approaches, help a volunteer, board member or donor who has name recognition in your community pen an editorial for the local newspaper spotlighting the special month and sharing positive ways your organization's mission relates to it.

- Ask volunteers to tell how serving your organization positively influences their lives. Sharing compelling volunteer stories is a great way to entice others to step forward.

- Interview your most effective and longtime volunteers. Ask them to share their most emotion-filled stories relating to the service your nonprofit provides. Share these stories with donors, staff, the community and potential advocates to engage readers in ongoing support of your mission.

- Remember that stories can be told in ways besides words. Collect images from photos shot throughout the year or create a storyboard that reflects the service and impact of your nonprofit to share with a broader audience.

35. Develop a Brochure Template That You Can Customize

Need a simple but cost-effective way to promote various involvement opportunities?

Develop a brochure template that can be used to create any number of brochures that describe your organization's different volunteer projects. Having a standard template with standard categories in hand means that you need only fill in the blanks to produce any number of in-house brochures to hand out, stuff in envelopes or otherwise target groups of would-be volunteers.

As an example, use a standard 8 1/2 X 11-inch sheet to create a folded three-panel brochure (many computer programs come with such templates ready for your modification). Folded, the front panel would include your agency's name, optional logo or line art and name of the particular project you're promoting. Unfolded, the inside would describe the program in detail, with the third panel used as a tear-off return form with your mailing address on one side and information to be completed by the volunteer on the other, so the volunteer need only tear it off, fill it out, add a stamp and drop it in the mail to you.

Some information in the brochure would remain the same regardless of the project/program being described, while other information would be tailored to that particular project/program, giving all your brochures a similar look people will come to identify with your organization.

To add two-color flair to your brochures, have preprints made in colored ink (and a paper style and weight of your choice) featuring information that will be identical regardless of brochure content (e.g., your organization's name, logo/line art and return address). When you need a brochure for a specific project, create the text unique to that program, format it to fit on the preprint, then run the brochure off on a copier, so the project-specific information is added in black.

36. Attract Single Working Parents as Volunteers

Single working parents may wish to participate more actively in volunteer activities, but feel unable to do so because of family and career responsibilities. Take their special circumstances into consideration by using techniques such as these to provide opportunities for single working parents to help your cause:

1. **Recruit teen volunteers to baby-sit younger children.** Develop a group of youth who are old enough to baby-sit children during meetings. Reward them with certificates or recognition. Not only will they become familiar with your organization at an early age, but parents can attend to business knowing that responsible youth are nearby caring for and entertaining their little ones.

2. **Give volunteers some supplies for a home office.** Some volunteers may have time to offer once they have fed, bathed and put their children to bed. Later evening hours may be the best time for them to accomplish their tasks.

3. **Offer them jobs that involve their children.** When you need signs or posters created, envelopes stuffed or other routine but crucial tasks, see if the parent of an elementary or junior high-age child wants the task. Older children may be eager to help paint, draw, sort mailings and other simple duties. Remember how easily children can turn work into fun. Many also are proficient with computers.

4. **Keep meeting attendance requirements reasonable.** While many volunteer organizations have fairly strong attendance requirements, think of important jobs that don't require a great deal of committee interaction, so the parent won't have concerns about arrangements. Two or three times a year, plan a meeting that is casual enough or in a location that children may attend without disrupting business, such as in a facility with a gymnasium where children can play supervised games while parents meet nearby.

5. **Provide plenty of valuable contact with a knowledgeable liaison.** When an experienced committee chairperson or liaison can keep single parents updated on important developments, or agrees to be available as a mentor for that volunteer, fewer meetings are likely to be necessary.

6. **Develop a "Grandparent" team to spend time with children.** Like many senior citizens' facilities have started grandparent programs with small children in churches or other organizations, see if older volunteers would like to have a story time or special activity with the children of your single volunteers that coincides with your group meetings.

7. **Write a press release about how you are helping single parents volunteer.** Once you have two or three plans established to accommodate single parents while they complete their assignments, write a press release telling media what those plans are and how they work. Those waiting for an opportunity to volunteer will be made aware of your efforts, and positive publicity may encourage wider media interest.

37. Seven Ways to Approach Religious Groups for Help

If you have more volunteer opportunities available than you have volunteers, explore ways to make your needs known through religious institutions.

By developing a system of broadcasting your message through churches and synagogues, you can win the attention of hundreds, perhaps thousands of potential volunteers over time.

Employ the following methods to build relationships with churches/synagogues and get your message out:

1. Create a mailing list of religious institutions in your service area. Send periodic notices for bulletin inserts, church newsletters or public worship announcements.

2. Schedule a series of visits to top congregation choices and speak during their worship service. Bring along someone served by your agency or institution if possible.

3. Host a program or reception for the clergy or lay leadership of area churches and invite them to assist in your recruitment efforts.

4. Regularly profile a church/synagogue in your newsletter or magazine that summarizes its community involvement efforts.

5. Just as you may list names of volunteers in your newsletter or annual report, be sure to include names of religious institutions that have provided volunteer assistance.

6. Ask existing volunteers to approach their congregations on your behalf.

7. Create a religious institution award to be presented annually along with your other volunteer awards.

38. Create a Win-win Situation With Corporate Volunteering Options

Corporate volunteering can be a win-win situation. Your organization can end up with a great group of volunteers, while employees can enjoy quality time together outside the workplace. But there are some things to keep in mind to make this partnership work.

Each year Zoo Miami (Miami, FL) sees an average of four to five corporate volunteer groups. When a company shows interest in a corporate volunteering opportunity, zoo officials work to come up with a specific program of activities for that group. "Basic tasks such as planting, painting, mulching, and hauling/spreading holding area materials work best. The projects change with our current needs, priorities and number of volunteers," says Tom Trump, the supervisor of horticulture at the zoo.

At Zoo Miami, corporations are encouraged to sign up for ongoing, periodic or one-time volunteer projects. "The projects vary with every group. They involve our horticultural, maintenance and animal science staffs," Trump says.

To make corporate volunteering a success, Trump says it's important to be well-organized and to brief the groups ahead of time, so they are prepared on the day of the event. He says it's also important to have personnel who can work effectively with volunteers.

Trump says companies usually hear about volunteer opportunities from other corporate groups and the Zoological Society of Florida. The zoo's website also includes a page dedicated to corporate volunteering. The page provides three volunteering options for businesses:

- **Adopt-a-Project** — "You can work with zoo professionals to determine a specific activity that your corporation can make your own, for example, a children's educational program or activity, the promotion and beautification of a particular animal exhibit or providing guides for traveling exhibits with a schedule that fits your needs as well as those of the zoo."

- **Hold a Corporate Zoo Day** — "Bring the whole gang together for a one-time Zoo Beautification day complete with a front entrance banner proclaiming (Your Corporation Name) Day at the Zoo! Enjoy a fun day of teamwork and camaraderie in a tranquil setting."

- **Link Your Corporate Donations to Your Community Service** — "If you are interested in making a corporation donation to Zoo Miami, you may want to consider linking your funds to your employees' volunteer service donating a specific amount for every hour volunteered."

Source: Tom Trump, Supervisor of Horticulture, Zoo Miami, Miami, FL. Phone (305) 251-0400. E-mail: TRUMP@miamidade.gov. Website: http://www.miamimetrozoo.com/volunteers. asp?Id=52&rootId=9

Recruitment Tip

If you have a new project to assign, who would you give it to: a busy person or someone with plenty of time on his/her hands? Although there is logic to the second choice, don't underestimate choosing the busy person. Busy people are oftentimes the ones who get things done.

39. How to Attract 100 Volunteers in 48 Hours

Do you ever find yourself needing lots of extra volunteer help on short notice?

Whether you need 10 extra volunteers immediately or 100 extras in a short time, here are tips to enlist help in short order:

1. Ask volunteers to call everyone they know. Use a calling tree to spread the word among your ranks.

2. Get board members into the act. While their primary responsibilities are hiring/firing CEOs and approving policy, they are also, in many cases, expected to do volunteer work.

3. Give the project the urgency or drama it deserves in messages to would-be volunteers and the media (e.g., "Be a part of history! Join our 'human chain' as we move our entire children's book collection to our new addition in record time!").

4. Ask employees to help and to recruit friends, family and associates, too.

5. Ask other volunteer-driven organizations if their volunteers could lend a onetime hand, knowing you may be called on to return the favor at some future date.

40. Publicize Volunteer Programs, Accomplishments to Attract Others

How often do you send volunteer-related news releases to area media? Don't miss an opportunity to place volunteer-related news. Doing so brings your cause needed visibility and is a valuable way to recognize your corps of volunteers.

Need some examples of volunteer-related news releases? Try these:

- New volunteer appointments.
- Election of officers with profiles.
- Feature stories of volunteers in action.
- Retiring volunteer profiles.
- Volunteers who have received awards.
- Intergenerational volunteer profiles.
- Volunteering couples' profiles.
- Stories of long-term volunteers celebrating anniversaries with your organization.
- Youth volunteers involved with your cause.
- Partnerships with businesses and their employees.
- An article including a list of your entire volunteer force to demonstrate your charity's community impact.
- A feature on a collaborative effort between your organization's volunteers and those of another.
- Volunteers who have made a significant financial contribution to your cause.

41. Develop Themed Recruitment Programs

If you could use a few extra volunteers, why not develop a recruitment theme aimed at particular groups? Need a few examples? Try any of the following:

1. **Siblings of Volunteers Day.** Sponsor a day that encourages siblings of existing volunteers to get involved.

2. **Give Us 30 Days to Prove Our Worth.** Approach a different church or synagogue each month and invite its members to select from among a menu of give-us-30-days-to-prove-our-worth involvement opportunities.

3. **Help Fuel Our Cause.** Select a day for existing volunteers to position themselves at existing gas stations in your community and sign up as many station customers as possible to donate an hour of volunteer time that's convenient for them.

42. Identify Recruitment Obstacles To Help Overcome Them

Challenged by not getting sufficient numbers of volunteers? It might be due to any of the following obstacles:

- Not knowing where to find them.
- Not breaking jobs down into small enough tasks.
- Denial of the need for volunteers.
- Few or no volunteer benefits.
- Having not defined what volunteers can do and how they can help make a positive difference.

Identifying obstacles to volunteer recruitment is the first step in determining how to overcome them and, ultimately, draw more participants to your volunteer ranks.

43. Pre-filled and Blank Forms 'Sell' Volunteer Slots

Online volunteer recruitment forms can encourage new and existing members and volunteers to share their expertise within your organization.

The Technical Association of the Pulp and Paper Industry (TAPPI) of Norcross, GA, accomplishes this through two new volunteer recruitment forms on its website that encourage more members — new and existing — to volunteer within the TAPPI ranks.

Serving more than 20,000 professionals in the paper, packaging and converting industry, TAPPI is currently testing the forms intended to encourage volunteer participation among members and identify skill levels as well as need within the TAPPI community, says Rich Lapin, marketing manager.

Lapin explains the purpose of the new forms:

Blank volunteer form (top right): This open-ended request to members allows potential volunteers to raise their hand to become involved, Lapin says. Areas such as experience level, location and division/committee are intentionally left blank for volunteers to complete. The form offers those new to the industry and recent college graduates the opportunity to participate readily within the organization by offering their new skills through volunteerism.

The form is also intended for use by division and committee leaders as a resource to identify current volunteer needs within their division and to place volunteers based on experience and skill levels within the organization. Once a potential volunteer completes this form, committee leaders review it to determine where the person may best fit within the volunteer realm of the organization.

Completed volunteer form (lower right): This form is intended to "sell" specific volunteer opportunities within the organization by offering detailed descriptions of volunteer posts. The form also guides division and committee leaders as they prepare for immediate volunteer needs. These detailed volunteer descriptions include specifics such as division/committee, volunteer title, number of positions available, time commitment, project type, experience level needed, job description and benefits for participating.

Most importantly, Lapin says, this form offers a posting date for the opportunity as well as a posting expiration date. A posting date indicates when the position first becomes available and the expiration date is tied to the term of service needed. This allows volunteer coordinating staff to track when a position completes its term of service or the time by which a new volunteer is needed for that office.

Source: Rich Lapin, Marketing Manager, Technical Association of the Pulp and Paper Industry, Norcross, GA. Phone (770) 209-7290. E-mail: rlapin@tappi.org. Website: www.tappi.org

44. Web Tool Boosts Online Recruitment

Think of it as a charity-focused Monster.com, combined with the scope of Craigslist, powered by a sophisticated search engine and personal customer service.

Bintro.com (New York, NY), a free website that matches individuals to job openings, business opportunities and nonprofits nationwide, relaunched in April 2010. The relaunch makes use of the latest semantics technology, says Richard Stanton, CEO, "which allows the website to draw a relationship between two people who make different statements, but want to get to the same end goal."

"For example, someone may say that he is looking for a group that focuses on 'environmental causes.'" Stanton explains. "Meanwhile, a charitable organization may describe itself as being dedicated to the promotion of 'green energy.' Semantic data allows us to recognize that a relationship exists between the keywords."

Officials with Grassroots.org (New York, NY), which provides other nonprofits nationwide with free technologies and resources to boost efficiency and productivity, used Bintro.com in 2009 to find new volunteers. A request using the tool asking for volunteers in web design and graphic design brought 55 leads.

"Bintro is a wonderful tool for nonprofit organizations in need of skilled volunteers," says Laura Benack, Grassroots.org interim executive director. Previously, Grassroots.org relied solely on Craigslist posts for volunteer recruitment, Benack says. "Bintro has helped us immensely by referring talented, skilled volunteers directly to our organization."

She gives Bintro.com high marks for customer service, too.

"Bintro's uniqueness lies in the personalized attention that each nonprofit receives," Benack says. "When we recommended Bintro to our members, 38 of them contacted Bintro, and each was guided through the process of finding volunteers by a Bintro team member."

Sources: Laura Benack, Interim Executive Director, Grassroots.org, New York, NY. Phone (800) 252-0015.
E-mail: laura@grassroots.org. Website: www.grassroots.org
Richard Stanton, Chief Executive Officer, Bintro.com, Hoboken, NJ. Phone (646) 736-0393. E-mail: rstanton@bintro.com.
Website: www.bintro.com

45. Timely, Friendly Contact Key to Recruitment

Making your volunteers feel appreciated from the first contact they have with your organization is critical to maintaining a roster of Good Samaritans ready to pitch in at all times.

No one knows that better than Suz McIver, director of volunteers at Midland Care (Topeka, KS). Because Midland Care volunteers deal with hospice patients, McIver says, burnout is a frequent problem, creating a constant need for new volunteers. She handles this by streamlining the process of welcoming new volunteers into the organization.

"The challenge is to get volunteer help in there as soon as we can," McIver says.

The effort to secure new volunteers is a team effort between McIver, a part-time staff member and a part-time clerical volunteer. They mail information packets to potential volunteers within 24 hours of initial contact and follow up with a phone call within a week. Next, McIver interviews the volunteers for placement. Persons who selected as volunteers undergo extensive training in sessions offered every three months.

McIver's advice for successful volunteer recruitment is to be flexible about volunteer opportunities and schedules. For example, Midland Care operates a resale store that volunteers may staff if they prefer not to work directly with patients. The organization also offers volunteer shifts on nights and weekends.

In addition, McIver recommends being open during the orientation process so that volunteer candidates know what to expect and can walk away if it's not for them.

Midland Care currently has 167 active volunteers and averages five volunteer inquiries each week, says McIver, who credits this high response to community awareness about Midland Care's mission, vision and values.

Source: Suz McIver, Director of Volunteers, Midland Care, Topeka, KS. Phone (785) 232-2044, ext. 410. E-mail: smciver@midlandcc.org

Recruitment Strategy

If you're looking to get the word out about your volunteer opportunities, you may want to start posting catchy listings on various volunteer-friendly websites. Writing eye-catching descriptions and posting them at viable sites creates a combination that is sure to fill your opportunities.

46. Tap New Volunteers by Following Who's Retiring

Do you keep track of who's approaching retirement at various businesses and organizations around your city? This can prove to be a great source of volunteers who find themselves finally having the time they want to help with worthy causes.

Maintain a tickler report of key businesses, schools and other organizations to contact at least yearly to determine who is scheduled or planning to retire in the near future.

After determining who's up for retirement, send a letter of congratulations at the time of retirement and share some opportunities for volunteer involvement with your organization. Indicate that you will be phoning the retiree within the next several days to follow up.

— Who's Approaching Retirement? —
Organizations to Contact Yearly

Business or Organization	Contact Person	Phone	Person(s) Scheduled to Retire	Retirement Date	Congratulatory Letter Sent	Follow-up Call Date	Comments

47. Volunteer Information Sessions Help Educate, Recruit

Whet potential volunteers' appetites with an upbeat, brief information session about helping your cause.

Five years ago, the Vanderbilt University Medical Center (Nashville, TN) began offering volunteer information sessions as a starting point for some of its 650 existing volunteers as well as persons interested in volunteering at the Monroe Carell Jr. Children's Hospital at Vanderbilt, Vanderbilt Medical Center and Vanderbilt Health – One Hundred Oaks, says Stephanie VanDyke, director of volunteer services at Monroe Carell Jr. Children's Hospital at Vanderbilt.

VanDyke says the sessions showcase hospital values, expectations and specific volunteer openings. In addition, they help educate potential volunteers about duties and expectations, and reduce costs for volunteer training by helping match recruits to appropriate volunteer tasks.

The training sessions feature a 15-minute video with interviews from current volunteers, an overview of the hospital and a look at the commitment and training that goes with being a hospital volunteer.

The one-hour sessions are offered one evening a month in January, March, May, August and September. VanDyke and Andrew Peterson, director of volunteer services at the adult hospital and clinics, say they see the highest attendance in August and September because many college students are available then. January is also another popular month because many people sign up to volunteer during the holiday season.

Interested volunteers are required to attend the information sessions and must register in advance. Peterson says they advertise the information sessions on the Vanderbilt website about four weeks before the session date. Posting the information any earlier, he says, can result in many people signing up, but then forgetting or losing interest. He adds that they have found that directing people to their website is the best way to advertise an upcoming session.

After the session, the attendees are given the opportunity to sign up for an interview, with about 90 percent of them doing so. Once the interview is complete, Vanderbilt works to have the new recruits in place within three to four weeks.

With the large number of interested volunteers, space limitations and the ability to follow up and schedule interviews in a 3-to 4-week time frame, organizers limit the number of attendees at each session. While some sessions have seen more than 100 people sign up, on average Vanderbilt has 50 to 60 people register for each session.

Sources: Andrew Peterson, Director of Volunteer Services, Vanderbilt Medical Center, Nashville, TN. Phone (615) 936-8871. E-mail: andrew.r.peterson@Vanderbilt.Edu
Stephanie VanDyke, Director, Volunteer Services, Monroe Carell Jr. Children's Hospital at Vanderbilt, Nashville, TN. Phone (615) 343-3692. E-mail: stephanie.vandyke@Vanderbilt.Edu. Website: http://childrenshospital.vanderbilt.org/

48. Appeal to Sports Enthusiasts

Try these techniques to attract more sports enthusiasts to your volunteer programs:

1. **Promote events that spark their interest.** For example, ask a company to sponsor your volunteers in a softball game. For every run that's scored, the company agrees to donate a certain amount of money.

2. **Offer your volunteers an incentive**, such as free tickets to a sporting event or a free round of golf. See if area golf courses or sports stadiums will donate the tickets.

3. **Keep up-to-date on big games.** Plan meetings and events around key sporting events, but make sure the event doesn't conflict with game time.

4. **Ask managers of local sports-related establishments (e.g., bowling alleys, sports bars, country clubs, ball fields, etc.) if you can post volunteer opportunities there.**

49. Create a Volunteer Prospect List

It's not unusual for development officers to create a list of prospective donors before soliciting funds. They research 10 to 15 prospects, and then narrow the list to the top two or three. Why not use the same approach for your volunteer organization?

Make a list of the volunteer opportunities available at your agency and determine what is expected of each position. Then you'll have an idea of the type of person needed to fill that job. Now, create a list of prospective volunteers for each position. As you make your list, think of the best person for the job. Narrow your list to the top two or three prospects, and then call those people and make an appointment for a specific time to talk.

Keep the list on file. Then as new volunteer opportunities become available, you can easily identify and contact the best prospects.

50. Goal: 100 Men, 100 Days

Three nonprofits embarked on a mission to sign on 100 male volunteers within 100 days.

Halfway through the campaign, the organizations signed on 53 new volunteers across the participating agencies — Big Brothers Big Sisters of the Central Piedmont (High Point, NC), Big Brothers Big Sisters of Greater Greensboro (Greensboro, NC) and Big Brothers Big Sisters Services, Inc. (Winston-Salem, NC).

Among all three organizations, female volunteers outnumber male volunteers two to one. At each agency, there are approximately 100 boys looking to be matched with a male big brother and 50 girls waiting for a big sister. Boys waiting for a big brother match are typically from single-parent homes that need a male adult to be a good example in their lives.

Girls within the Triad North Carolina agencies are matched within six months, while boys wait one to two years for a match.

The difference in the number of male to female volunteers was the premise behind the 100 Men in 100 Days campaign that took place from July 24 to Oct. 31, 2009.

"Men have a special opportunity to impact the lives of boys in our community using the proven model of Big Brothers Big Sisters," says Melissa Wilson, vice president of operations at Big Brothers Big Sisters of the Central Piedmont. "We want to engage men who have a desire to be a friend, to have fun and make a difference. We hope our 100 Men in 100 Days campaign highlights the number of ways men — and

women — can become involved in this movement."

To target males for your volunteer efforts, Judi Saint Sing, volunteer coordinator with the Winston-Salem organization, suggests the following:

- Go to where the men are. Host presentations where you'll find male volunteers with varied backgrounds (e.g., churches, businesses, restaurants and sports centers).

- Seek young, male volunteers at fraternities and at college events.

- Advertise in male-specific publications, on TV channels with a high demographic of male viewers and radio stations that feature programming for male listeners. Find mediums that focuses on male subscribers, including local publications' sports pages.

- Ask current male volunteers to recruit their male colleagues.

- Ask for incremental volunteer efforts. Big Brothers Big Sisters asks that volunteers — both male and female — commit to just one activity per week to begin their initial efforts, an approach that's particularly good for busy professionals.

Source: Melissa Wilson, Vice President of Operations, Big Brothers Big Sisters of the Central Piedmont, and Judi Saint Sing, Volunteer Coordinator, Big Brothers Big Sisters, Inc., Winston-Salem, NC. Phone (336) 724-7993. E-mail: jsaintsing@bbbsnc.org.

51. Volunteer Support Adds Enchantment to Royal Event

Special volunteers helped make the Princess Party for the Children & Families of Iowa (CFI) of Des Moines, IA, a special event that enchanted attendees while raising money for the nonprofit.

The October 2009 Princess Party event drew more than 600 attendees for a day of princess-like pampering. Nearly 50 volunteers offered assistance with activities including meeting real princesses, getting autographs, creating princess crafts, having glamour makeovers, enjoying breakfast and games, and watching a special screening of the princess-themed movie, "Enchanted," at a local theater.

Susan Joynt, CFI events manager, shares techniques to recruit appropriate volunteers for a similar event:

❑ Call on a local university sorority to get volunteers willing to dress as princesses and ask them to volunteer in the craft area of your event.

❑ Ask a local birthday party business to provide princess volunteers and costumes that will enchant guests.

❑ Don't forget to ask real royalty to volunteer. At the CFI event, Miss Iowa and Miss Teen Iowa were asked to attend, adding to the royal theme.

Source: Susan Joynt, Events Manager, Children & Families of Iowa, Des Moines, IA. Phone (515) 697-7961. E-mail: susanj@CFIOWA.org. Website: www.givetocfi.org

52. Form a Volunteer PR Committee to Reach Out to PR Pros

Your organization's board has a well-rounded, respected public relations committee of volunteers. Each member is ready to use his/her skills and contacts to help enhance your charity's image and educate the community about your services.

Now what do you do with all of this talent? How can you respect these individuals' time while still reaping maximum, continuous benefit? Here are some worthwhile ways to put your PR committee to work:

- **Ask them to speak to various groups about your organization.** Provide them with brochures, videos and contact information when they are guest speakers in the community.

- **Invite them to scout for sponsors for your events.** Committee members may be aware of other business execs who, for their own public relations reasons, want to sponsor a worthy project or event. Ask if they would be willing to contact three potential sponsors or in-kind donors each month.

- **Encourage regular creativity with group meetings.** If your public relations committee meets at least quarterly, ask each member to arrive with a promotion idea for one of your programs.

- **Request yearly image assessments.** These committee members will hear feedback about your organization that you, as paid staff, may not hear. Ask for an oral or written assessment from each, pointing out image strengths and weaknesses.

- **Invite committee members to write letters to other community leaders and businesses.** Make the letters friendly and informative without asking for money at this time. Your members can write it in their own words, tell the reader why they value involvement in your organization, and invite them to do the same.

- **Assign thank-you calls to your committee.** Your supporters will enjoy getting regular calls from friendly ambassadors who simply want to express appreciation for past contributions, not ask for more donations at this time.

- **Charge members to serve as ambassadors at large.** Word of mouth is one of the most effective ways to spread good news about your organization. Request that each member tell one or two friends a week about one of your programs or services.

- **Invite them to look for promotional opportunities in their neighborhoods.** Each member of the committee is loyal to certain retailers — grocery stores, gas stations and dry cleaners. Would the stores that your committee members patronize make brochures available or post some announcements for your cause?

- **Give committee members responsibility for developing promotion ideas,** volunteering for the job(s) they would enjoy doing themselves, or suggesting the name of a new volunteer to assist.

- **Assign committee members to serve as your media spokespersons at appropriate times.** When it's time for a radio or television interview about your institution or a special event, ask one of your most skilled committee members to be your spokesperson. Enthusiastic words from a volunteer may be more meaningful to the audience.

53. Take Advantage of Group Gatherings

Whenever you host any type of group gathering — a seminar, an open house, a meeting, etc. — use those captive opportunities to invite attendees to become involved as volunteers.

Produce a large poster you can display next to the registration table or in some other visible location that includes an invitation to volunteer and lists specific ways in which individuals can help. In addition to the display, have an easy-to-complete form — one that mirrors your poster — that attendees can pick up and either take with them or complete and turn in while they are at the function. Here's an example:

> We Welcome Your Involvement!
>
> Here are just a few of the ways in which you can become involved with Negas Medical Center:
>
> - Assist in the Gift Shop
> - Conduct tours
> - Give presentations to civic groups
> - Serve on our Community Relations Committee
> - Help with a special event
> - Share your computer skills
> - Join the Negas Auxiliary
> - Host seminars, workshops
> - Staff the reception desk
> - Serve as an ambassador
> - Assist in fund development
> - Help at our annual telethon
>
> - Serve as a period driver
> - Visit with and assist patients
> - Help with mailings
> - Contribute your writing skills
> - Help sell items to generate needed funds
> - Assist with office duties: filing, records management, etc.
> - Assist with outside landscaping and beautification efforts
> - Serve on our Planned Gifts Committee
> - And so much more!

54. Corporate Partnership Blends Volunteerism, Fundraising

The Columbia Humane Society (CHS) of St. Helens, OR, has forged a corporate bond with local restaurant Burgerville (St. Helens, OR). The two organizations celebrated Partnership Night, where guests enjoyed a family meal out at Burgerville with 10 percent of the proceeds benefiting the humane society.

Christine Braud, a CHS volunteer, answers questions about this partnership:

How did CHS form a partnership with Burgerville?

"Burgerville has been making an ongoing effort to support community nonprofits for several years. To continue a strong bond, we make a point to communicate regularly and honor Burgerville's requests and restrictions regarding the event, such as the number of volunteers we should have and the tasks we are to perform."

How has the event changed or improved since the beginning of this partnership?

"We use Burgerville's display cabinet to highlight our nonprofit and to feature photos of shelter animals that are available. We attempt to reach more people each year and have progressed from using just flyers to promoting the event by adding information to local reader boards and sending blanket e-mail messages to our lists."

What are the top ways that you promote and make this event successful?

- "Once a date is determined for the event, we immediately advertise in our newsletter and online."

- "We print mini-flyers that the restaurant places in their takeout and drive-thru bags. This gets the word out to multiple customers in a fast, efficient fashion."

- "We also create coloring sheets for children that advertise our event and place copies on tables inside Burgerville."

- "At the event we provide several volunteers who help deliver food, chat with customers about CHS, clean tables, sweep the floor, empty trash and more. We also set up a table and sell some of our fundraising items."

Source: Christine Braud, Volunteer, Columbia Humane Society, St. Helens, OR. Phone (503) 397-4353. E-mail: cbraud@opusnet.com. Website: www.columbiahumane.org

Recruitment Exercise

At your staff meeting, pose this question: "Why should anyone want to volunteer for our organization?" The discussion that follows should provide some answers about unique volunteer opportunities with your organization — ones you can use in recruitment efforts.

55. For Volunteers With Flexible Schedules, Look for Freelancers

Seek out freelancers within your community to fill volunteer posts that require flexible hours. A freelancer is someone who is self-employed or contracts independently for a company, oftentimes working from a home office. Freelancers work in a wide array of industries including writing, translating, consulting, graphic design and others.

Rest assured there are likely a number of freelancers within your community who can offer your nonprofit a flexible schedule for volunteering.

Consider posting or locating freelancers at these websites:

- Freelancers Union – www.freelancersunion.org
- iFreelance – www.ifreelance.com
- Freelancers – www.freelancers.org
- FreelanceSwitch – www.freelanceswitch.com
- All Freelance – www.allfreelance.com

56. Drive Would-be Volunteers to Your Website

Is your website up-and-running? If that's the case, begin using it to attract potential volunteers. Here are three examples of how you can draw visitors:

1. **Offer a free e-mail newsletter on your site.** Help visitors learn more about your cause and the many ways in which they can become involved and rewarded as a result.

2. **Participate in listservs.** Include your URL — website address — in your signature when you participate. That way, every time you answer a question or offer a suggestion, everyone seeing your message can click on your URL to learn more about your organization.

3. **Put your URL (website address) everywhere** — business cards, brochures, letterhead, advertising, envelopes and more. Expose your website to as many would-be visitors as possible.

57. Engage Boomers to Strengthen Volunteer Efforts

The nation's 72 million baby boomers now comprise about 23 percent of the United States' population. And as the leading edge of this group enters their mid-60s, finding ways to interest them in your volunteering opportunities becomes increasingly important.

The Minnesota Association for Volunteer Administration (MAVA) of Maplewood, MN, has developed 12 best practices to effectively engage the boomer population into your volunteer force:

- Understand this group's deep-seated need to have impact and use that understanding in all facets of how you involve them as volunteers.
- Focus the volunteer interview on learning the prospective volunteer's passions, helping determine if your organization is the right place to realize the impact the individual wants to have and collaboratively designing the volunteer role.
- Offer a wide choice of volunteer opportunities in all aspects of organizational operations.
- Include some short-term and seasonal volunteer positions to align with volunteer availability.
- Offer skills-based volunteer opportunities to maximize what volunteers can bring to the organization.

- Develop position descriptions that are engaging and demonstrate impact.
- Move volunteers into leadership roles. Be open to project ideas that volunteers propose.
- Develop appealing recruitment messages and work through your organization's networks. Cultivate prospects and be highly visible on the Web.
- Reframe traditional views of volunteer supervision. Identify high-potential volunteers and prepare them to take on additional responsibility.
- Also reframe volunteer recognition to better respond to the value they place on having impact and being lifelong learners.
- Be an instigator for organizational change. Start small in a part of the organization open to innovation and market successes to colleagues in other parts of the organization.
- Create systems to monitor changes in volunteer expectations; become a learning organization that adapts to the changing needs of volunteers.

Source: Mary Quirk, Volunteer Resources Leadership Project Manager, Minnesota Association for Volunteer Administration, Maplewood, MN. Phone (651) 255-0469. E-mail: mquirk@mavanetwork.org. Website: www.mavanetwork.org

58. Encourage Young Volunteers at High School Volunteer Fairs

Representatives from the Kalamazoo Valley Museum (Kalamazoo, MI) attend local high school volunteer fairs to draw young talent who will likely stay with their nonprofit long-term. The museum, operated by the Kalamazoo Valley Community College (Kalamazoo, MI), seeks to develop cultural, historical and scientific literacy through innovative exhibits, special exhibitions, planetarium programs, educational programs and family events.

"We try to get students as volunteers then keep them throughout high school, and many still volunteer through college," says Annette Hoppenworth, programs coordinator of the Kalamazoo Valley Museum. "Many of our local schools have volunteer fairs for students and invite organizations to present volunteer opportunities available."

Catching the attention of teenagers at a youth volunteer fair can pose challenges. Hoppenworth offers tips for attracting youthful volunteers at your next volunteer fair:

✓ **Giveaways.** Offer candy, T-shirts from your nonprofit's previous events or pencils with your name and logo.

✓ **Photos.** Display pictures or photobooks of volunteers in action. Teens like to see what they'll be expected to do and like to see other teens in action.

✓ **Contact cards.** Create cards that allow interested volunteers to simply fill in their name and contact information to receive information about your volunteer opportunities. Hoppenworth says her prior attempts to get volunteers to complete applications at volunteer fairs netted little response, but at one fair, she received 95 completed interest cards, with 88 of those becoming volunteers at the museum.

✓ **Explain benefits of volunteering.** Emphasize the benefits that high school students will receive by aligning themselves with your organization, including summary letters of their hours and letters of recommendation toward college applications.

Source: Annette Hoppenworth, Programs Coordinator, Kalamazoo Valley Museum, Kalamazoo, MI, and Kalamazoo Valley Community College, Kalamazoo, MI. Phone (269) 373-7997. E-mail: ahoppenworth@kvcc.edu. Website: www.kvm.kvcc.edu

59. Reach Out to Professionals

Tapping professionals in your community to volunteer their skills at your nonprofit can be a rewarding experience for the volunteer and your organization. To encourage professionals to volunteer for your cause:

1. **Send local professionals an invitation** to your next event. Ask them to get a feel for your organization and to consider ways they can donate their special talents while attending the event.

2. **Define a limited time** for professionals to volunteer so they do not feel taken advantage of or overwhelmed. This specific request could allow the professional to fit the volunteering time into his/her busy schedule.

3. **Begin a partnership** with a professional on a professional level. Hire the professional to work at an event, requesting up front for him/her to donate a percentage of time or portion of product to your nonprofit. This could make for a win-win scenario for both the professional and your cause.

60. Turn to Senior Corps For Ready, Willing Volunteers

If your nonprofit is seeking a quality group of senior volunteers to assist in your efforts, consider contacting Senior Corps at www.seniorcorps.gov.

Senior Corps is an arm of AmeriCorps (Washington, D.C.) and is a broad-reaching volunteer organization that includes specialized departments of senior volunteers serving their communities.

Senior Corps volunteer branches, divided by service, are:

* *Foster Grandparent Program* connects volunteers 55-plus with children and young people with exceptional needs. Senior volunteers mentor vulnerable children in the U.S.

* *Senior Companion Program* unites volunteers 55-plus with adults in their community who need assistance with day-to-day living. Companions help on a personal level by assisting with daily life tasks such as shopping or light chores.

* *RSVP* unites 55-plus volunteers with service opportunities in the community, matching the volunteer's skill set with community need.

61. Letter Aims at Involving Civic Groups

Do you have projects that would benefit by having a group of committed volunteers in charge of getting them staffed and carried out? Since many types of civic organizations and other groups include community service as part of their mission, why not contact these groups two or four times a year and share some ways in which they can become involved?

Having a system in place to accomplish this will ensure the organizations get asked to help and will serve as a continuing reminder to them that you welcome their group participation. The format also provides these groups the opportunity to view and select a project that appeals to them.

Develop a letter similar to the example below and send it to your community's civic groups, religious institutions and area associations. Include a bounce back that they can complete and return. You can develop a database of these groups by contacting your local chamber of commerce, reviewing the Yellow Pages and newspapers.

Sample letter and return card directed to area civic clubs and groups.

Dear (Name of Club President):

We could sure use your help!

Doesn't matter if you have five or 500 members. We'll work with you to come up with a volunteer project that matches your wants with our needs.

Want to learn more? Here's just a sampling of group projects in need of your assistance:

❑ **Annual cookbook sale.** Every three years we publish a cookbook as a way to generate needed funds. Your organization's members could help us sell this year's cookbook.

❑ **Transportation.** It would be helpful if we had a dedicated group of volunteers who are on call for transportation of those in need.

❑ **Campus clean-up and beautification.** Twice a year we make a group effort to clean up our campus and beautify it in various ways — planting flowers, shrubs and trees; painting and more. It's always a good time for those who participate.

❑ **Mentoring.** Many of our young people could use someone in their lives who takes a special interest in them. We would love it if one organization chose this as a special project.

❑ **Safety watch.** There are times when it would be helpful to step up security around campus. Your members' assistance would provide a valuable service during designated times throughout the year.

These are but a few of the opportunities for club/group involvement with our agency. If your group would be willing to assist — or interested in learning more about how a particular program works — please complete the enclosed form and return it to us. I will get back to you with answers and/or additional details.

Thanks for considering this special request!

Sincerely,

Gayle A. Westerhoff
Volunteer Manager

LEND A HAND

Name of Club/Organization_____
Number of Active Members _____
Contact _____ Phone _____

We would be willing to assist you with the following project(s) _____
_____

We might be interested in assisting with the following project(s) but want to learn more first_____
_____

❑ We have a project of our own that we could like to suggest as a way to help your organization. Please contact me to discuss it.

Here are some community involvement projects with which our club/group has assisted:

Organization Served_____
Project Description _____

Organization Served_____
Project Description _____

Organization Served_____
Project Description _____
_____

Recruitment Idea

With the end of the year approaching, many people start to focus on New Year's resolutions (e.g., volunteer more). This may be a great time to connect with area businesses, churches, schools, gyms, etc. Why not ask them if you can decorate a wall or bulletin board in their building with photos of volunteers and info about your agency? This is an excellent way to both recognize and recruit volunteers.

62. Five Ways to Find Techie Volunteers

Having qualified technical volunteers can be a great benefit to a nonprofit. Those individuals can perform a variety of tasks including setting up a website, maintaining existing computers and installing new equipment. But where can you find these talented individuals?

Here are some suggestions for locating technical volunteers.

1. Contact a national volunteer matching program such as **www.volunteermatch.com** or **www.techsoup.org** for technical volunteers. Many cities also have similar programs which do volunteer matching. (New York and Seattle are two cities with such programs.)

2. Get permission to put a notice on a bulletin board or be included in an in-house newsletter at a local high-tech company.

3. Check with computer science teachers at area high schools, colleges or technical schools for qualified students who may want some actual experience designing websites and working on similar projects.

4. Contact engineering organizations on those campuses and ask them to make an announcement at one of their meetings about your need for volunteers.

5. Look for meetings of computer societies or clubs in your area and contact them about how to find technical volunteers.

63. Recruit Couples to Volunteer

Do you have volunteer projects that reach out to couples?

Inviting couples to volunteer gives them the opportunity to be together as they serve a common effort, offers a ready-made comfort level of working with a familiar face and strengthens their relationship.

You benefit by getting two volunteers with each request instead of one.

To initiate a program that encourages couples to volunteer:

1. **Identify volunteer opportunities that most appeal to couples.** Survey employees to identify couples' opportunities. Create a checklist of projects ranging from simple to complex — filing, staffing front desk, co-chairing an event, team phoning or solicitation, serving as hosts or tour guides, etc.

2. **Develop a plan to market volunteer projects to couples.** Consider an ad program that reaches out to couples and lists volunteer opportunities. Recruit a couple to lead your couples program and enlist others. Do a feature story on a volunteer couple to illustrate the rewards of couples' volunteering.

3. **Work with couples to keep them invigorated.** Once you have couples involved, find out which projects they find most rewarding and weed out those they do not. Ask couples what can be done to support their work.

4. **Identify unique ways of recognizing couples' efforts.** Host periodic appreciation events for all volunteering couples. Offer special bus trips or discounts to restaurants. Make volunteering as a couple attractive to those who have not yet stepped forward.

64. Target Computer Specialists

Rather than recruiting computer generalists as volunteers, go after individuals with computer specialties. By doing so, you not only involve more people in the life of your organization, you also find individuals who have expertise in particular areas.

In fact, you can spell out those specialties in a brochure or your newsletter or carefully placed ads (e.g., college/university newspapers, school bulletin boards, corporate in-house newsletters).

Some computer-related skills you can go after might include:

- Computer/software acquisition decisions
- Website design
- Setting up and monitoring an online auction
- Data entry
- Website maintenance
- Program development
- E-newsletters, e-mail communications
- Computer networking
- Publication layout and design
- Word processing
- Training staff/volunteers how to use software
- Database management

You might even want to involve a computer-literate volunteer in deciding what kinds of positions to fill first.

65. Nurture Spouses' Involvement

Are you giving your volunteers' spouses and significant others opportunities to become involved as volunteers?

These spouse recruitment techniques might be just what the doctor ordered:

- Get to know more about the interests of volunteers' spouses, then explore which tasks or projects you have that would match those interests.

- Offer a onetime, short-term project for volunteers and their spouses — one that mixes fun with work.

- Try the carrot-and-the-stick method: Any volunteers and their spouses who participate in a designated volunteer project will receive two movie tickets.

- Invite spouses to your annual volunteer recognition event. As you're making volunteer awards, ask all spouses to stand and be recognized for their supporting roles. Point out the volunteer sign-up cards at every table and that you would welcome the spouses' greater involvement in your organization.

66. Find the Hidden Talents Among Your Volunteers

Recruiting an unskilled volunteer force to help out at a one-time special event is often much easier than finding certain professionals whose specific skill sets align with just what you need to help your organization grow. How should your recruiting efforts differ from one type of volunteer to the other?

Jennifer Iscol, director of North Bay Celiacs (Santa Rosa, CA), which offers support to persons with celiac disease and gluten intolerance, discusses the different recruitment methods her organization employs to attract all levels of volunteers:

How does your recruitment of highly skilled, executive-level professionals differ from the ways you recruit "unskilled" volunteers to man special events?

"For special events, I just put out an e-mail to our general membership and take the volunteers who respond. Sometimes they show up, and sometimes they don't — but a few will really surprise me with their dedication and hard work. Those folks I may then attempt to get to know better by e-mail or in person at our events. I observe their communication style, skills and professionalism. When I feel confident that someone might make a good match for our needs, I'll approach him or her by e-mail to begin a discussion."

Are there tricks you've developed to figure out the hidden talents of as many of your volunteers as possible?

"Talented people rarely jump right in and offer themselves up. They become a member, observe our organization and my leadership skills, and slowly reveal more about their own skills and how they might contribute. It can take a few months or even a few years for them to come forward and accept a serious organizational role.

"As for their not-so-hidden talents, I find those using Google. I Google all of our new members for a variety of reasons, including safety. Sometimes I find that they are in a profession that would be a good match for our needs. From there, it's a matter of approaching them appropriately and respectfully, but usually waiting until they offer a bit of information about themselves. Of course, if they use their business name, title, website, etc. in their correspondence, then I feel that asking about their profession and volunteer interests are fair game."

How do you learn what potentially important contacts a volunteer has without coming across like you're only interested in a volunteer for the people he/she may know?

"People with great contacts are going to reveal themselves slowly after they've established trust. I don't know any way to shortcut this process without becoming a person I don't want to be!"

What's the most successful way to approach a volunteer with requests for his or her time, expertise, skills, contacts, etc.?

"If I can explain with enthusiasm and honesty how we would love to have them join our volunteer efforts, and how their particular skills would be helpful, they almost always respond in a positive way, even if they cannot help at that time. It's also all about contacting or talking with them directly. People are more likely to ignore a group e-mail and less likely to decline a personal request by phone or e-mail."

Source: Jennifer Iscol, Director, North Bay Celiacs, Santa Rosa, CA. Phone (707) 824-5830. E-mail: info@northbayceliacs.org. Website: www.northbayceliacs.org

67. Make Board Member Recruitment, Evaluation Top Priorities

Finding and evaluating key board members should be a priority for any nonprofit. Board members are instrumental in molding and adhering to the fundamental mission of the nonprofit they serve.

The Bridgespan Group (Boston, MA) is a nonprofit organization that assists philanthropic and nonprofit leaders with advice on strategy and executive search. Since its inception in 2000, the Bridgespan Group has relied on an active group of board members to help steer the organization's development.

Wayne Luke, partner and head of executive search, offers the following advice for recruiting and vetting board members suited to your nonprofit:

- ❑ **Strategic Priorities.** Consider key strategic priorities and what skills or expertise a board member will need to help your organization achieve them. Also, while having a celebrity on the board can have its value, it is the degree of engagement and willingness to invest time that will be the greatest contribution of any board member, regardless of celebrity status.

- ❑ **Diversity.** Consider diversity among board members. Have a diversity goal before you recruit. This goal can include gender, ethnic and racial balance, as well as geographic location and other factors.

- ❑ **Meeting Basic Requirements.** Ask the following key questions of potential board members as part of your organization's early due diligence:

  - ✓ Can you fulfill our board's fiduciary and legal oversight responsibilities?
  - ✓ How have you demonstrated a passion for organizations like ours?
  - ✓ Do you have the time to sit on our board?
  - ✓ Can you meet our fundraising requirement (if your organization has one)?

- ❑ **Cultural Fit.** Besides meeting specific requirements, it's important to determine whether a board candidate will fit with the organization's culture. So evaluating for cultural fit — whether the candidate connects with the mission, the organization's board members and staff, its work style, etc. — is important to the recruitment process. A good way to ensure that a candidate is properly vetted is to enlist the help of your board's difference makers, its most engaged and active members. This will help you gain a perspective on the candidate through the lenses of your most-involved board members.

- ❑ **Board Roles.** Finally, after talking to a candidate, the group overseeing the board recruitment process should discuss what specific board role the candidate could play. Be intentional about the role the candidate could fill and the value he or she would bring to the team.

Source: Wayne Luke, Partner and Head of Executive Search, Bridgespan Group, Boston, MA. Phone (617) 572-2686. E-mail: Wayne.Luke@bridgespan.org. Website: www.bridgespan.org

68. Make the Most of Introductory Visits

How can you go about pulling together a group of volunteers in regions outside of your immediate area? What does it take to assemble a group of volunteers for your cause when you're unfamiliar with that community's or region's citizens?

If you're charged with starting chapters or advisory committees throughout your region or the nation, here are some ways to recruit able-bodied volunteers:

- First, review existing records to see who, from that community/region, is on your mailing list and may be familiar with your organization's work. Then, work through them to assemble a group of potential volunteers for your arrival.

- Set appointments with officials who may be able to help introduce you: The local chamber of commerce, organization heads whose work may have a connection to the work of your organization, the local RSVP chapter and others.

- Set up and publicize a public meeting or reception for interested citizens to attend and learn more about your cause and their potential involvement in it.

- Offer to present a program to any civic organizations holding regular meetings during your scheduled visit. Following your program, distribute a volunteer sign-up form and literature about your organization.

69. Retired Military Members Make Great Volunteers

Volunteers come from all walks of life, including some perhaps unexpected places. Take the military, for example. Those who have spent their adult life serving in the military and are now retired offer nonprofits some unique qualities.

Teamwork — The military is known for the concept of working as a team to get the job done — a great quality for any volunteer to have.

Leadership — Those who have risen through the ranks of the military have been given leadership roles. Part of the requirement for achieving higher rank in the military is to attend leadership schools and perform as a leader.

Discipline — Former military members are used to focusing on a job and getting it done.

If your organization is near a military installation, get permission to put flyers about your group around the base. Also, contact any local military groups such as the American Legion or the Veterans of Foreign Wars (VFW) and let them know about volunteer opportunities at your nonprofit.

70. Community Partnerships Boost Volunteering

From helping at a local food pantry to repairing bicycles for area youth, students at the University of Wisconsin (Madison, WI) make a major impact on the community through its Badger Volunteers program.

Started in 2008 with four community partners and 40 students volunteering each week, the program currently boasts 50 community partners and more than 400 students.

"I think the growth has been so immense because the reciprocal partnership is so strong," says Megan Miller, Badger Volunteers coordinator. "Students love the program because we handle the logistics, and they have the opportunity to volunteer with friends. Community partners love that the students are showing up consistently and forming that strong relationship with the site; everyone has something to gain and share.

"In an exit survey, 95 percent of Badger Volunteers say they will continue to serve the community after their Badger Volunteers experience."

In order to make it easier for students to find the volunteer activity that works best for them, the Badger Volunteers program sorts the opportunities into four categories:

- ❏ Environment
- ❏ Youth and Education
- ❏ Health and Aging
- ❏ Hunger and Homelessness

"We try to offer a variety of service options for students so when we add new sites we are looking to fulfill the community's need while offering unique service opportunities that will help students grow," says Miller.

School officials let students know about the program in many ways, says Miller, who notes that word of mouth is the most effective. School officials also give presentations at student dorms, post flyers around campus, send out weekly newsletters, hold a volunteer fair every semester and list volunteer opportunities on Facebook and Twitter.

There is no academic credit given to students who participate, but each student receives a T-shirt and the opportunity to make valuable connections. "For students who may have just moved to Madison, Badger Volunteers makes it easy for them to get involved in their new community," says Miller.

Since many college students don't have a car, helping them find transportation to the volunteer site is important. If the volunteer site is located off the bus route or out of walking or biking distance, a volunteer transportation program gives free cab rides to students who are Badger Volunteers.

For volunteer managers looking to recruit students, Miller says don't hesitate to contact schools directly. "Helping college students volunteer is what we do and we have various channels to reach out to them," she says. "We also help faculty find placements for their students in service-learning classes."

Miller says the first place they look when trying to help place student volunteers is www.volunteeryourtime.org, an online database of volunteer opportunities in the area coordinated by the United Way of Dane County (Madison, WI).

Source: Megan Miller, Coordinator, Badger Volunteers, Madison, WI. Phone (608) 262-0731. E-mail: vista@morgridge.wisc.edu. Website: http://www.morgridge.wisc.edu/programs/bv/index.html

Recruitment Tip

If your organization is in need of a helping hand from high schoolers, consider approaching your nearest Key Club — a youth organization sponsored by Kiwanis International. Key Club exists on more than 50,000 high school campuses, primarily in the U.S. and Canada, with members providing more than 10 million service hours annually. Contact Key Club International to locate the club nearest you.

71. Help Your Potential Chair Visualize What's Expected

Sometimes volunteer coordinators can become so desperate to find anyone willing to chair a committee or spearhead a project that they fail to reveal everything involved for fear the person won't accept the job. Unfortunately when that happens, the chairperson often becomes discouraged, and the job doesn't get carried out as it should.

When recruiting someone to head a committee or project, you're much further ahead if you share the project in its entirety the moment you make the ask. By providing a project or committee summary, such as the example shown at right, the individual can either accept or reject the position knowing exactly what is involved. And if the person chooses to accept the job, he/she will be far more successful having known up front what's involved.

Share a committee or project summary sheet like the one shown here to help a would-be chairperson visualize the size and scope of what will be expected.

PROJECT SUMMARY:	Wine-tasting Event Clean-up Committee
Scheduled Event Date:	June 11 — 6 pm to 10 pm
Event Location:	Elks Club
Anticipated Attendees:	200-300

Responsibilities:

✓ Recruit 12-20 individuals to help clean up immediately following the event (10 pm to midnight) and return rented or borrowed items the following day.

✓ Meet with committee one time prior to the event to go over responsibilities.

✓ Touch base with Elks Club personnel to establish contact.

Time Requirements: 6 to 9 hours inclusive

72. Seniors Boost Volunteer Efforts

Persons age 65 and older make up 85 percent of the 550 volunteers for The City of Huntington Beach (Huntington Beach, CA).

Diane Swarts, volunteer services coordinator, specifically targets persons of retirement age to volunteer, noting that she finds members of this demographic to be valuable assets to Huntington Beach's program.

Senior volunteers serve many roles in the Huntington Beach region, from performing senior well checks, to singing at senior living facilities, to delivering meals and driving other seniors to appointments. In 2009, volunteers gave 36,000 rides to those in the community's aging population.

Swarts shares five tips for recruiting and retaining senior volunteers:

1. **Schedule to fit senior lifestyles.** Swarts recruits seniors by assuring them that her volunteer program will not interfere with their golf, grandchildren or travel. Enlisting the help of many volunteers allows for greater scheduling flexibility and offers volunteers the freedom to take time off when needed.

2. **Prepare a strong substitute force.** Swarts has a group of 125 to 150 volunteers who act as substitutes for her regular, long-term volunteers.

3. **Enlist feedback when changes arise.** Senior volunteers take volunteering seriously and want to offer feedback when program changes arise. Swarts collects feedback from a volunteer focus group of 10 to 12 to obtain viewpoints on proposed changes. She also polls volunteers at group meetings on pending changes.

4. **Create staff mentoring.** Once trained, volunteers are assigned to specific departments led by one of eight full-time staff, creating a tight-knit group of persons serving the same cause.

5. **Facilitate follow-up.** Swarts' volunteers know that if they write concerns about clients in a specially designated binder, staff will check on that client within 48 hours. Offering volunteers this outlet for helping clients gives them peace of mind and solicits a stronger feeling of commitment.

Source: Diane Swarts, Volunteer Services Coordinator, City of Huntington Beach, Huntington Beach, CA. Phone (714) 374-1544. E-mail: dswarts@surfcity-hb.org. Website: www.huntingtonbeachca.gov

73. Four Ways to Find Last-minute Volunteers Over the Holidays

If you find you're shorthanded this holiday season and need to find some episodic volunteers fast, try looking in these places:

1. **College campuses.** Solicit help from college students who stay on campus over the holidays. Should you need a volunteer with particular expertise, look to the heads of college departments for names of students likely to assist.

2. **High schools.** Solicit the help of high school counselors and staff to identify students likely to assist in volunteering over winter break.

3. **Partner with another nonprofit.** Work out a volunteer sharing system to solicit help from regular volunteers at another nonprofit. Work with another local volunteer manager to share your volunteer lists for recruiting last-minute help.

4. **Mentoring organizations.** Ask a mentoring organization to connect you with mentors and mentees who could work together to help you while strengthening their bond.

74. Point Out All Volunteering Benefits

People volunteer for different reasons. That's why it's important that your recruitment literature points out all of volunteering's benefits. Review your volunteer recruitment information. Make sure it mentions that volunteering allows an individual to:

✓ Favorably impact a community's quality of life.

✓ Make professional contacts.

✓ Gain recognition.

✓ Learn or develop skills.

✓ Receive free or discounted perks.

✓ Gain work experience.

✓ Strengthen leadership skills.

✓ Socialize.

✓ Build self-esteem and confidence.

✓ Improve health.

✓ Meet new people.

✓ Enjoy cultural, educational and/or recreational opportunities.

✓ Feel needed and valued.

✓ Make a difference in someone's life.

✓ Express gratitude for help received in the past from an organization.

75. Look for Innovative Ways to Recruit Volunteers

Looking for volunteers can be simple using the right techniques. Try these innovative volunteer recruitment techniques to bolster your volunteer base:

- **Work volunteer opportunities into public presentations.** When presenting a speech about your organization or appearing on a panel, use the opportunity to mention your agency's need for volunteers. Members of the audience are there to hear you speak and therefore interested in your organization. Ask the members of the audience to complete a sign-up sheet if they are interested in volunteering.

- **Tap volunteer organizations for volunteers.** Look to service-minded membership organizations within your community for volunteers who will assist your organization as a group. Your local Junior League, Boy or Girl Scout troops, Lions Clubs or business organizations, for example, are likely to volunteer in groups for upcoming events. Seek them out.

- **Seek to bring in young people.** Get in touch with high schools and the heads of college departments to solicit youthful volunteers for your cause.

- **Turn to employers.** Talk to personnel directors of companies, explaining in detail the volunteer opportunities available at your nonprofit. Ask if they will assist you by referring retirees and employees to volunteer at your nonprofit.

76. Use Public Access TV to Reach New Audiences

Recruiting volunteers for your organization could be as easy as turning on the television.

Nan Hart, executive director of RSVP and the Volunteer Center (Rutland, VT), has been taking her plea for volunteers to the airwaves for more than 12 years by taping more than 100 shows that have aired on her local channel. Hart says, "It's amazing how many people watch local public access stations. I estimate that we have gained over 150 volunteers who indicated that they saw the show and contacted us as a result."

The Federal Communications Commission requires every cable company to have a public access station that provides free equipment and a studio to the public. Most public access stations have staff available to help run the camera, but in some cases, you may need to recruit your own camera operator.

"If possible don't make the show time sensitive," Hart suggests. "This way the interview doesn't sound dated," she says, noting that creating a timeless piece will allow you to use it as a promotional DVD, on your website and in other ways to promote your volunteer organization.

Also, keep your audience in mind. Hart says having a show on a public access channel will usually result in middle age and elderly volunteer recruits.

Hart tapes a new 30-minute show about once a month.

The local cable access company airs that spot about 12 times a month. Each spot includes an interview.

She shares some suggestions of questions to ask during each interview:

- ❑ Can you please share a brief description of the organization?
- ❑ What is it like to volunteer at the organization?
- ❑ What types of volunteer opportunities are available?
- ❑ What is your organization's contact information?
- ❑ What type of time commitment is required?
- ❑ Can you share some personal stories of volunteers' experiences?
- ❑ Is travel involved?

"After watching the interview, people should have a good sense of what it takes to volunteer at the site," Hart says.

Providing contact information is important when doing a public access show. During her show, Hart uses a graphic with contact information for her organization as well as the group she interviews. In addition, showing a video or slide show can also help generate interest in volunteering.

Most public access channels also provide a free bulletin board listing of community events and opportunities. Many also post the information from the bulletin board and the shows they air on their website to communicate volunteer opportunities with people who don't have cable.

To find out more about your local public access channel, contact your local cable provider, the chamber of commerce or your local public access station directly and tell them you're interested in starting your own show.

Source: Nan Hart, Executive Director, RSVP and the Volunteer Center, Rutland, VT. Phone (802) 775-8220, ext. 101. E-mail: rsvprutlnd@aol.com. Website: www.volunteersinvt.org

Make the Most of Your Camera Time

Nan Hart, executive director of RSVP and the Volunteer Center (Rutland, VT), is an on-camera veteran with more than 100 public access interviews to her name.

For people less experienced in front of the camera, Hart shares tips for creating an effective TV interview spot:

- ✓ Write a brief opening to introduce the show and your guest.
- ✓ Once the interview begins, pretend you are having a normal conversation with the person you are interviewing.
- ✓ Relax. Tell your guests to look at you (the host) during the interview. Don't pay attention to the camera.
- ✓ Practice in front of a mirror.
- ✓ Have a sense of humor.
- ✓ Personalize the interview. Tell stories that relate to your community.
- ✓ If you don't feel quite ready for TV, give a local radio show a try, as this can be a good warm up to TV.

Recruitment Tip

Your local paper makes an obvious choice for listing opportunities for volunteer participation, but don't overlook local shopper publications as well. Most shoppers are delivered free to all homes, making your message more accessible to those who may not subscribe to the local newspaper.

77. Online Site Helps Connect With College Volunteers

Looking for a go-to spot on college and university campuses to recruit volunteers?

Karen Partridge, communications manager, Campus Compact (Providence, RI), says they partner with more than 1,000 colleges and universities to help establish relations with community organizations across the country.

"Campus Compact helps build strong campus-community ties while providing volunteer managers a resource to recruit volunteers on campus," says Partridge.

Volunteer managers can utilize www.compact.org, to access the following resources:

- **"Promise of Partnerships."** Partridge says the "Promise of Partnerships" is a volunteer manager's guide to tapping into local colleges and universities' resources.

The publication offers advice on making the right contacts, planning effective partnerships and working with students and faculty. The book also features tips, checklists and best practices.

- **Program models.** Visitors can access more than 700 established program models used by colleges and universities to create relationships with their community agencies.

- **Online volunteer opportunities list.** Community-based organizations can post their volunteer opportunities at: www.compact.org/opportunities/volunteer. Some 9,800 college students, faculty and campus community service directors visit the site weekly.

78. Major Delivery Company Helps Deliver Volunteers and Grants

You know them best as the men and women in brown uniforms who deliver packages to your door. But UPS is delivering more than just boxes to some volunteer-based organizations. In 2010, UPS' global workforce donated more than 1 million volunteer hours, says Ronna Branch, spokesperson for the UPS Foundation (Atlanta, GA).

"We are a doorstep company," Branch says. "We are literally in neighborhoods across the country and we see firsthand the needs in these communities."

Through UPS' Neighbor to Neighbor program, UPS employees log in to an online database to record time volunteering and post volunteer opportunities to share with coworkers. The site is for UPS employees only, but Branch says if you know a UPS employee they can go onto the database and post any volunteer opportunities they hear about. "We have a close relationship with the United Way, therefore, many of our volunteer connections start there. However, we encourage employees to donate their time to whatever organization they choose," says Branch.

Every year one of UPS' 400,000-plus employees receives the Jim Casey Community Service Award, which recognizes outstanding community service. Finalists must be nominated and the winner is chosen by a panel of UPS employees, UPS retirees and community leaders. The winner is flown to Atlanta, GA to receive the award and featured in a video on the UPS blog. In 2010 the winner was Terry Brown, a UPS human resource manager in Omaha, NE, who volunteers 66 hours a month at various organizations including the Ronald McDonald House, Open Door Mission,

Embrace the Nations and the NAACP.

Grants are also available to the organizations where UPS employees volunteer. The winner of the Jim Casey Community Service Award receives a $10,000 grant for the charity of his/her choice. Every year each district also selects employees who volunteer more than 50 hours annually at one organization to receive a $10,000 grant for that organization.

While the company encourages its employees to volunteer year round, October is UPS Global Volunteer Month. UPS Global Volunteer Month started in 2003 and since then thousands of UPS employees in more than 50 countries have helped at food banks, schools, shelters and other organizations. "We encourage all our corporate offices to set up a group project in October," says Branch.

To learn more about recruiting UPS employees as volunteers contact your local UPS Customer Center and talk to the community service person on staff. And before you do, make sure you're contacting a UPS Customer Center and not The UPS Store. Branch says while The UPS Store may participate in community service projects, they are independently owned and operated and are not part of UPS corporate volunteer efforts and recognition programs. Visit ups.com to find your closest UPS Customer Center or e-mail foundation@ups.com with any questions.

Source: Ronna Branch, Global Reputation Management, Spokesperson, The UPS Foundation, Atlanta, GA. Phone (404) 828-4393. E-mail: rcbranch@ups.com. Website: UPS.com/foundation

79. Create Volunteer Continuity With a Yearly Recruitment Plan

Think Outside the Box When Drafting a Recruitment Plan

It's important to be creative when forming a volunteer recruitment plan. Kim Deer, interim executive director of the Okmulgee County Family Resource Center (Okmulgee, OK) came up with these novel approaches to recruiting volunteers:

- Call your local utility company, bank, car dealership, etc. and request space at the bottom of their monthly statement for a volunteer recruitment ad.

- Host a gathering for your current staff/volunteers where the price of admission is one potential new volunteer.

- Ask a local flower shop to insert a brochure with all the flowers delivered on Valentine's Day or Mother's Day, the two biggest delivery days of the year.

- Ask your local newspaper to interview a current volunteer. This allows readers to more easily relate to your cause.

- Call your local school board and request permission to deliver brochures to teachers' mailboxes.

- Ask a local sports association to advertise your program on an outfield billboard or scoreboard.

- Request that volunteer recruitment ads be posted in church bulletins.

- Request that volunteer recruitment ads be posted in the menus of local restaurants.

- Sponsor a youth sports team. A logo brings a lot of attention at sporting events.

- Negotiate an opportunity for current volunteers to work a concession stand at a local event. Word of mouth is a great recruitment tool.

- Create a fan page on a social networking site such as Facebook or Twitter.

- Create a website for your program and keep it up-to-date with activities and announcements.

Deer says, "No matter what recruitment method is used, the message must be compelling and convey to the audience that the opportunity is well worth their efforts."

Recruiting volunteers is a yearlong process. That's why the directors for the Court Appointed Special Advocates (CASA) program at the Okmulgee County Family Resource Center (Okmulgee, OK) came up with a yearly volunteer recruitment plan.

"We have been pleased with the results, as we have increased volunteer recruitment by 31 percent over the past two years," says Kim Deer, interim executive director of the center.

Deer offers these tips for creating a plan:

- Set realistic goals and time frames.
- Know the role of your organization.
- Know the demographics of your targeted recruitment area.
- Evaluate progress of the recruitment plan periodically.
- Be flexible. Recruitment needs often change for an organization.

When putting together a volunteer recruitment plan, Deer says it's important to look at the trends in your community and be aware of what has and hasn't worked in the past. "We always make sure we know exactly where every volunteer came from and how they heard about us," she says.

Throughout the year Deer monitors progress by using an Excel-based program to track recruitment and retention of volunteers. "In addition to tracking new recruits, it's important to monitor when and why volunteers are leaving your organization. If you find you get off target with your recruitment goal, re-evaluate what went wrong and find a way to change it," she says.

For the CASA program in Okmulgee, the volunteer recruitment plan goes hand-in-hand with wider organizational goals and objectives. "We always look at how many children we plan to serve and how many volunteer advocates are needed by looking at what was used for the previous year," says Deer.

The final copy of the plan is printed and reviewed with everyone in the agency, including board members, staff and volunteers. Deer says a plan will only work if you and all your staff believe in it and in what your organization is doing.

Source: Kimberly Deer, Interim Executive Director, Okmulgee County Family Resource Center, Inc. Okmulgee, OK. Phone (918)756-2549. E-mail: casaokm@sbcglobal.net. Website: http://www.ocfrc.org/

Content not available in this edition

80. Don't Forget About Your Local Volunteer Center

Need volunteers — fast? Don't forget about your local volunteer center or similar agencies. Volunteer centers can frequently match willing and talented volunteers with nonprofits in need. Here are a few key questions to consider:

✓ How do you find volunteers?

✓ What kind of information do you keep on file? Skills? Interests? Hours available? Reason for volunteering?

✓ How up-to-date is your database of volunteers?

✓ How do you match organizations with volunteers?

✓ What percent of organizational requests for volunteers are filled? How quickly are requests filled?

✓ How can my organization work with you effectively?

81. Pick From a Fresh Crop Of Volunteers

Do you need volunteers to perform landscaping or plant-related duties?

Tap your county's Master Gardner program to fill the need.

Master Gardeners, located in every state, are required to perform 40 to 50 hours of volunteer service after their initial training to receive their certification. To keep their certification current, they must continue to volunteer every year.

If the volunteer service is plant-related, it qualifies. Master Gardeners can help care for flower beds or public gardens, give talks about plant care, raising vegetables or designing a landscape, or just answer persons' plant-related questions. Contact your county extension agency or visit www.ahs.org/master_gardeners/index.htm

82. Tips to Recruit and Retain the Best Volunteer Drivers

Volunteer drivers are an important volunteer resource for area communities. Volunteer drivers oftentimes assist transportation-dependent members of society by helping them run medical errands, by delivering meals or by transporting those in need for any other purpose.

At Tri-CAP Transit Connection & Volunteer Driver Program (Waite Park, MN), volunteer drivers are a critical component to the services they provide.

Linda Elfstrand, Tri-CAP transportation director, offers her tips on recruiting and retaining volunteer drivers:

• Ask current drivers to recommend friends or family members; coordinate efforts with your local United Way or RSVP programs; post opportunities at your organization's website or post a classified ad in your local newspaper.

• Offer thorough training. Tri-CAP volunteers receive a three-hour initial orientation followed by a three-and-a-half hour class on child passenger safety. Refresher training is offered in half-day in-service opportunities.

• Arm volunteers with information about how to handle

unusual situations. Tri-CAP volunteer trainees are asked to consider various scenarios and how to properly respond. Examples can include a passenger asking to make extra stops or bring extra people not on the manifest; the passenger displays inappropriate behavior during the trip; or the passenger sharing information about their home life such as abusive relationships.

• Offer an emergency number to volunteers. Also, encourage them to call the home office if questions come up on the road.

• Offer reimbursement benefits. Tri-CAP asks volunteer drivers to use their personal vehicles while driving, but reimburses drivers for their mileage. This benefit has allowed the organization to retain their trained volunteers.

• Include volunteer drivers in organization celebrations, regular office communications and special events.

Source: Linda Elfstrand, Transportation Director, Tri-CAP Transit Connection & Volunteer Driver Program, Waite Park, MN. Phone (320) 257-4445. E-mail: Linda.Elfstrand@tricap.org. Website: www.tricap.org

83. Involve Your Community's Classic Car Club

How in the world could members of a classic car club be of volunteer assistance?

Here are six possibilities, for starters:

1. Ask if the club would provide transportation, so your volunteers can represent your organization in local parades.

2. Offer to host a car show on your facility's grounds and use the opportunity to promote volunteer opportunities.

3. Get club members to allow you to offer a chauffeur-driven night out on the town in their showcase vehicles as a prize or perk to deserving volunteers.

4. Invite a club representative to give a presentation about classic cars to your volunteers during one of their social get-togethers.

5. Call on the club to offer fun rides to those you serve (e.g., children, students, seniors).

6. Ask the club leadership if they would consider organizing a fundraiser with proceeds going to strengthen your volunteer programs.

84. Volunteer Incentives for Those Who Recruit New Volunteers

Volunteers who bring new recruits into your organization offer valuable people skills that demand special recognition from your organization. Without the contagious enthusiasm of those who can bring new volunteers into the ranks, it would be a great deal more difficult for you to concentrate on expanding your programs and missions.

Offering volunteer recruiters regular awards, incentives and recognition for their efforts may encourage others to look for new volunteers, too. Try any of these ideas:

- Ask local businesses to help donate items for a Recruiter of the Month gift basket.

- Offer reserved parking at your facility and branches if space permits.

- Hold an annual tea or picnic for volunteers who have brought in new volunteers.

- Present a traveling trophy to go to the top recruiter each month.

- In monthly club notices or newsletters, consistently name the volunteer who has brought in the most new volunteers.

- Give volunteers a different lapel pin for each new volunteer they recruited — they will love lining up the pins and telling people how they earned them.

- Provide volunteer recruiters with gift certificates to your organization's gift shop, cafeteria, local popular restaurants or video rental store.

- Offer bonus hours or credits that count toward the volunteer recruiter's goals.

- Give the top five recruiters sets of complimentary tickets to your annual gala event.

- Design bumper stickers or window decals for volunteers who sign on new volunteers.

Recruitment Technique

Want to get an invitation to volunteers out to a big segment of your community at little or no cost? Contact local banks to see if they would agree to include a small insert in the monthly statements they send to customers

85. Targeted Recruitment: Finding Daytime Volunteers

Need 9 to 5 volunteers? They do exist, you just need to know where to find them. These daytime volunteers can provide a tremendous source of help to your regular workday efforts.

Here are obvious and not-so-obvious places to look for these valuable daytime contributors:

- Homemakers
- Teachers and professors (during summer months)
- Students
- Self-employed
- Weekend workers
- Salaried persons who set their own schedules
- Retired/semi-retired
- Wealthy persons
- Disabled
- Unemployed
- Evening shift workers
- Release-time employees

86. Tap Volunteer Expertise With Pro Bono Consultant Program

Encouraging persons to share their professional expertise to benefit your organization on a volunteer or pro bono basis could save your organization hundreds or even thousands of dollars each year.

Oftentimes when you think of such pro bono services, legal work comes to mind. But Michelle Birnbaum, the pro bono consultant program coordinator at the Montgomery County Volunteer Center (Rockville, MD), says legal work is just a small part of the pro bono services people are willing to donate. "If you can think of a consulting service, there is usually pro bono work available," she says.

Pro bono consulting services can include:

- Accounting
- Information technology (website redesign, graphic design)
- Marketing
- Grant writing
- Fundraising
- Organizational management
- Social media marketing
- Budgeting
- Human resource projects
- Program evaluation

Birnbaum says that when representatives of nonprofit organizations approach her with project requests in the hopes of engaging a consultant on a pro bono basis, she works to match those requests with pro bono consultants who have come to the volunteer center. In doing so, she says, she has learned it is important to make sure the staff and board of the nonprofit organization are trained and ready to work with a consultant.

"In order for it to work, everyone needs to be open to consultant work," says Birnbaum. "The nonprofit world and the business world are very different. It's a bit of a culture shock. We want to make sure the groundwork is laid before the consultant takes on the project. If the nonprofit board and staff aren't willing to listen to, or go forward with, what the consultant suggests, the project will likely not be successful."

Birnbaum says professionals are usually willing to commit to 30-, 60- or 90-day projects. "We don't solicit projects that are expected to last longer than three months," she says. "Whether it's a website redesign, marketing or grant writing activity, most of these volunteers are looking for short-term, well-defined projects where they can make a significant impact."

To seek out persons to donate professional services, Birnbaum says, "Reach out within your network. You'll be amazed at what people will donate. Don't be afraid to ask for more than just raffle prizes. Ask for in-kind services as well."

Websites Connect With Pro Bono Consultants

Looking for pro bono consultants in your area? Check out these sources:

- ✓ Local chapters of various professional service provider associations
- ✓ http://catchafire.org/ (New York City area)
- ✓ www.taprootfoundation.org (San Francisco, CA; Chicago, IL; Los Angeles, CA; New York, NY; Washington D.C.)

Source: Michelle Birnbaum, Pro Bono Consultant Coordinator, Montgomery County Volunteer Center, Rockville, MD. Phone (240) 777-2605. E-mail: probono@montgomerycountymd.gov. Website: www.montgomerycountymd.gov/mcgtmpl.asp?url=/content/volunteer/probono.asp

87. Create a Recruitment Video

Creating a recruitment video is a unique way to grab the attention of potential volunteers and members. Follow these simple tips for creating a recruitment video that will draw viewers to your nonprofit:

1. Create a video that includes unique features about your nonprofit after interviewing a veteran and new volunteer or member on camera.

2. Add background music and be sure the audio is clear and captivating.

3. Time the video for three to five minutes. Because you'll be posting the video to your website or social media sites, such as Facebook, you'll want to keep it brief, yet poignant.

4. Add visuals in your video clip that show the people you serve or your membership in action.

5. Have your volunteer or membership manager briefly share an invitation to join your organization as a volunteer.

6. Using video software such as imovie or Movie Maker, add graphics and fading breaks between interviews and captions to visuals to create a recruitment video clip you can share online, in e-mails and in public presentations about your organization.

88. Use Speaking Engagements To Recruit Volunteers

While flyers and websites play a key role in volunteer recruitment, nothing beats the human interaction of a face-to-face ask. That's why in-person speaking engagements play an important role in recruitment.

Do you head a nature conservancy organization? Offer to speak to community groups about environmental protection and sustainable agriculture. Work for a local symphony? Offer guest lectures for arts-focused lifelong learning classes. Such steps provide opportunities to introduce yourself and your cause to dozens of potential volunteers.

89. Formal Invitation Grabs Volunteer Prospects' Attention

Finding it difficult to get the attention of would-be volunteers? Send a formal invitation.

Formal invitations — particularly those that are hand-addressed — are generally the first items that get read as recipients review their daily mail.

Why not use a formal invitation, complete with RSVP, that requests the honor of their volunteer presence? Invite responders to attend an open house to meet your board and other volunteers, then tour your facilities.

Your invitation's RSVP could even include a listing of project preferences for the individual to identify.

THE STAFF AND BOARD OF DIRECTORS
OF THE MONSON
COUNTY HUMANE SOCIETY
REQUEST YOUR PRESENCE AT AN

OPEN HOUSE
THURSDAY, JANUARY 5, 2012
5 TO 7 PM

TOUR THE FACILITIES
VISIT OUR LOVEABLE "CLIENTS"
AND
EXPLORE VOLUNTEER OPPORTUNITIES

❖ ❖ ❖

LOCATED AT 5TH & MCCLAY STREETS
HARRISON, ARIZONA

__ I (We) plan to attend the Open House at the Monson County Humane Society, Thursday, Jan. 5, 2012.

I (We) would like to learn more about the following volunteer opportunities:

❏ Animal care ❏ Facility upkeep
❏ Membership ❏ Transporation
❏ Special events ❏ Ambassadors
❏ Clerical duties   ❏ Adoption
❏ Presentations ❏ Publicity
❏ Other _____

❏ I (We) can't attend, but would like to learn more about volunteer opportunities at Monson County Humane Society.

❏ I (We) cannot attend or volunteer at this time.

Name(s): _____

_____

Use this sample to create your own agency-specific formal invitation.

90. Places to Drum Up New Volunteers

Looking for additional volunteers? Whether you intend to place an ad or communicate your needs in other ways, don't overlook any of these options:

- Senior centers
- Yellow Pages
- Radio PSAs
- Newspaper
- High schools
- Government offices
- Civic organizations
- Others' websites
- Court-ordered community service programs
- Corporate newsletters
- Cable television announcements
- Posters in business establishments
- Independent living complexes
- Chamber of commerce
- Volunteer recruitment fairs
- Classroom presentations
- Lapel pins worn by existing supporters
- Bulletins at churches, synagogues and other places of worship
- Gathering places — laundromats, coffee shops, libraries, university commons
- Messages on giveaways: bumper stickers, shirts, hats, etc.

91. Unusual Places to Advertise

Pressed for more volunteers? Maybe you and your staff should brainstorm about new places to advertise for help. To get the wheels turning, here are some unusual advertising venues:

- ✓ Tabletop ads in bars.
- ✓ Bulletins distributed on car windshields at large sporting and entertainment events.
- ✓ Brochures in the waiting areas of auto service and tire businesses.
- ✓ Bulletins in teachers' lounges, gyms and wellness centers.
- ✓ Brochures at the information desks of large corporate buildings.
- ✓ Handouts distributed at high-traffic hiking, biking and walking trails, busy street corners and subway entrances.

92. Identify Projects Volunteers Can Do From Home

Get more volunteers involved in your cause by providing them with tasks they can do from their homes. By developing such a checklist of activities, you can both accomplish more and take an important first step toward getting more people engaged with the work of your organization.

Here's a checklist of some activities volunteers can work at from the comfort of their homes:

- Proofing
- Data entry
- Writing, editing copy
- Signing letters
- Assembling packets
- Making phone calls — announcements, recruitment, reminders, solicitation, follow-ups
- Wrapping
- Producing crafts, artworks, carpentry projects
- Sewing, mending, cooking, baking
- Counseling and mentoring
- Giving lessons and serving as study aids
- Responding to e-mail messages
- Developing and/or maintaining a website

Recruitment Technique

One way to recruit volunteers for hard-to-fill spots is to be up front about the nature of the work. Remember the Peace Corps' motto: "The Toughest Job You'll Ever Love." It worked for them.

93. Recruit Through Foursquare

The mobile application Foursquare offers ways to market events or recruit volunteers.

Users check in to report their location and post why they like a certain place. They rely on Foursquare to connect with friends and learn about new places.

Go to www.foursquare.com to become a Foursquare user and add your nonprofit, so other users can find it, learn ways to volunteer or be aware of events. As you become more proficient with using Foursquare, add tips about your nonprofit, including details on upcoming events.

Finally, create a meet-and-greet, volunteer recruitment or other event specifically for Foursquare users in your area.

94. Holiday Event Requires Specialized Volunteer Recruitment

Renewal House (Nashville, TN), which assists families affected by addiction, offers a special activity for 35 volunteers during each holiday season called Adopt-a-Family.

Families from Renewal House are adopted over the holidays by volunteers who either assist with cash donations so a staff member can shop for the family's holiday presents, or receive a copy of the family's wish list and shop for the family within a budget.

Individual holiday adoptions are available for a $75 gift and families, a $225 donation. Volunteers who do their own shopping wrap the gifts and return them to Renewal House by Dec. 15 to be distributed to families in need.

Lisa Harkins, development director, offers the following tips for finding the right volunteers for a similar type of episodic volunteer opportunity:

- Seek out social groups who can get together to help a family in need such as a book club, tennis group or other volunteer-friendly group in your community.

- Youth groups are especially enthusiastic about the chance to buy and wrap gifts.

- All it takes to volunteer is the desire to want to make a difference in the lives of others. In particular, work with local business people who can fill this need.

Source: Lisa Harkins Development Director, Renewal House, Nashville, TN.
Phone (615) 255-5222. E-mail: lharkins@renewalhouse.org.
Website: www.renewalhouse.org

Website Encourages Volunteers to Put Individual Talents to Work

The staff at Renewal House (Nashville, TN) use the organization's website to encourage volunteers to assist the nonprofit's mission of serving families affected by addiction.

At the website (www.renewalhouse.org), volunteers are encouraged to design their own volunteer program. Under the Volunteer section is the wording, "Bring your talents to life by creating your own special project for the women and children of Renewal House."

"We have many volunteers who bring their passions to teach our clients about different careers," says Lisa Harkins, development director. "We also have financial planners, exercise trainers, nurses and health experts come speak with women to help improve their lives."

To help volunteers find their place in your volunteer organization, Harkins says:

✓ Help volunteers identify a passion that has changed their life and help them focus on teaching others to benefit from that experience.

✓ If volunteers are in careers they love, ask them to share them with your clients.

✓ Volunteers who cannot identify their special skill to share should be coached by staff to identify it or choose from other options available at your nonprofit.

Lightning Source UK Ltd.
Milton Keynes UK
UKOW06f2121020913

216389UK00008B/193/P